The Back Up Plan

Alice Judge-Talbot

The Back Up Plan

CORONET

First published in Great Britain in 2018 by Coronet
An Imprint of Hodder & Stoughton
An Hachette UK company

1

A CIP catalogue record for this title is available from the British Library

Hardback ISBN 9781473689602
eBook ISBN 9781473689619

Typeset in Sabon MT by Hewer Text UK Ltd, Edinburgh
Printed and bound in Great Britain by Clays Ltd, Elcograf S.p.A.

Hodder & Stoughton policy is to use papers that are natural, renewable
and recyclable products and made from wood grown in sustainable
forests. The logging and manufacturing processes are expected to
conform to the environmental regulations of the country of origin.

Hodder & Stoughton Ltd
Carmelite House
50 Victoria Embankment
London EC4Y 0DZ

www.hodder.co.uk

To Elfie and Hux

CHAPTER ONE

The First Shag

I wake up in a single bed somewhere in north London, a stranger's warmth close to mine. The man is unfamiliar: his body is small and slight, very different from the large all-encompassing frame of my 6 foot 3 inch ex-husband. The snoring man beside me has a profile I don't recognise, the angular edginess a contrast to the soft bearded face I'm used to.

Whoever is lying next to me farts in his sleep, an act that in my marital bed would result in conspiratorial giggles, a result of the inevitable closeness that comes from a ten-year partnership. But in this alien situation I feel so much second-hand embarrassment from the stranger's flatulence in the presence of my own nakedness that I want to simply die from shame.

Anything would be preferable to what I know is going to happen next, an act I've abstractly read about in women's magazines for the last decade but have never had to experience myself. I'm going to have to speak to this strange man I just had sex with. In fear I clutch his musty brown covers to my naked chest as he rolls over in the early morning light. The sheets are silky to touch but not in the high-thread-count way, the sateen-hotel-sheet way. They're silky because they're threadbare polyester, the sheets of a twenty-something man who uses his bed only to sleep, shag and fart in.

I make myself glance around the rest of the room, getting my bearings and plotting my exit.

When I retell this first post-marriage sexual encounter anecdote to my friends I'll describe the one-room flat as a studio apartment; in reality calling it a bedsit would be generous. The battered shopfront facade hides a narrow grimy room with exposed rusty pipes, a stained futon and 90s-era TV/VCR combo the main feature of the living space. My head is two feet away from the filthiest oven I've ever seen, the kitchen it resides in comprising a couple of ancient cupboards and a two-pan electric hob – I wonder if this area is something an estate agent would optimistically term a 'kitchenette'.

I'll tell my friends the man was an artist (unemployed), a musician (needed a hair-wash), with a dazzling personality to match (I'd had six pints so didn't care). I'll reimagine the story to be romantic, with the guy a starving artist type: the Christian to my *Moulin Rouge* Satine.

In reality the whole situation feels more *Trainspotting* than *Moulin Rouge*.

Past the kitchen-cum-bedroom is the bathroom, a rusty mildewed affair with a tiny shower and a stained toilet bowl. I daren't look at the floor, knowing the sight of someone else's filth soon to touch my bare feet might send me over the edge and into the realm of hungover gagging.

This situation is a fitting metaphor for the downwards trajectory that my marriage, which ended four weeks ago, has taken.

At this moment I feel further away from my once-loving marriage and its 2.4 children than I've ever been.

Never have I wanted to be home so much. Home in my warm and comforting suburban semi with my children and soon-to-be-ex-husband, sitting on my IKEA sofa among baby walkers and wooden musical instruments, making a cup of tea in my floral-themed kitchen before going to bed in my comfy cotton sheets. Though home had felt like the most oppressive thing to me at the end of my marriage, at this moment there is nothing I crave more than my life of secure monotony and mediocrity.

The farting turns into grunting as the stranger next to me rolls again, his single bed restricting movement so much that his entire body lies flat against mine. My feet to his. His chest to my back. Knees locked like a jigsaw. His breath on my neck smells like last night's beer and teeth that haven't been brushed in too long.

As his hands snake round to grope at my chest I feel a hardness in his crotch. I am proud of my breasts: until two months ago I've used them to feed my eight-month-old son and they are still plump with breast milk, but in this situation having a stranger's hands on a part of my body that feels so explicitly like it belongs to my child feels wrong. I'd obviously felt different wearing my beer goggles last night but at this moment his hands are the last thing I want on my body.

I wriggle out of his sleepy grasp.

'Good morning!' I chirp brightly, mimicking a confidence and friendliness I don't feel.

'Hi,' he says, looking only a fraction as bewildered as I feel. 'Sleep well?'

'Like a baby!' is my ironic answer, as I hope my toddlers have slept better than me tucked up in their beds at home.

I nervously chatter as I search for a way to get out of bed while covering my modesty, realising far too late that my clothes have been slung on the other side of the room. He remains lying stationary, head propped up on one elbow as he intently studies my bare backside while I burrow around his belongings, desperately hunting down my sensible mum-tum-covering Marks & Spencer knickers.

I've never before been the type of woman who spends her bank holiday Sunday morning rummaging around in a stranger's things looking for her knickers: sure, I've chortled along with those stories of my friends and their sexual adventures, thinking they were so fun, so free-spirited, so edgy. And then I would go to my marital bed with my dependable husband in our dependable home, thanking whichever deity exists that my life was a little less fun, free-spirited and edgy. I liked it that way.

The woman I really am is the one whose overly large underwear lives in a perfectly organised drawer in the countryside, not in a mildewed corner of a bedsit. The woman who (admittedly begrudgingly) crafts with her kids (does anyone ever enjoy glitter?), goes to baby groups in chilly church halls; the one whose idea of a special treat is a food shop at Waitrose. The one who shares life with an ambitious yet charming and supportive husband, raises two perfect kids, meets friends for coffee before returning home to cook a healthy meal full of hidden vegetables for her family.

I'm the woman at the toddler group with the well-turned-out kids and a family car. I'm happily married, happy to be a mother. I'm you: only I'm not. Not any more.

The First Shag

I grew up in a happy family. Two parents, one brother, an infinite amount of love. Dad went out to work for a bank every morning while Mum stayed at home, made us cakes and picked us up from the school bus stop. With the government's 5 A Day campaign in full force, we snacked on carrot sticks and apple slices in front of *Byker Grove* – the edgiest thing we were allowed to watch on TV (I haven't felt the urge to go paintballing since) – went on holidays to Center Parcs and the Cornish coast and took day trips to National Trust properties. I spent teenage years counting down the days until I'd replicate my parents' marriage myself.

Which was why I thought I'd struck gold when I walked down the aisle at the age of twenty-three with the man I thought was the love of my life.

Will and I had met when I was eighteen and at university. Convinced that This Was It, we moved in together after six weeks, sharing a new-build flat in the centre of Nottingham with a swimming pool in the basement, a facility I could only have imagined having in my wildest dreams when I was a teenager fantasising about what adulthood might look like.

Having grown up with the Pony Club and shandies at the village pub as the cornerstone of my social life, I felt like I'd reached my own pinnacle of grown-up maturity with Will as my boyfriend. He was my boss at the nightclub where I worked behind the bar, a manager with lofty aspirations for a career in dance music promotion. We fell in love deep and hard, creating a bond of friendship and understanding that I thought would be impossible to beat. When he asked me to marry him after nine months I was beyond thrilled, even more so a couple of weeks later when he presented me with a diamond ring to make it official.

We married four years later at the Old Marylebone Town Hall, shrugging off thoughts of the famous failed marriages that originated there – Liam Gallagher, Chrissie Hynde. Will had quickly risen up the career ranks to become promotions manager at a new London superclub and I was working as a marketing manager for a mega-cool Shoreditch-based magazine. Making our union official at that point felt like the icing on the cake: we had the whole world at our feet.

Our marriage didn't get off to the most auspicious start. We'd decided to get wed in January for the sole reason that it was cheap, though having been engaged four years with no wedding date agreed, the topic of marriage had become tension-filled. I'd always dreamed of a country house wedding, a summer reception in a slightly sweaty white marquee, but in our skint and fun-loving early twenties, beer and living expenses were much higher on the financial agenda than saving to pay for a three-course meal for 150 of our closest friends and relatives.

Which was why one evening shortly before Christmas, when we'd once more rowed about our lack of impending nuptials and dwindling bank account, I stamped my foot and said we needed to 'just fucking get on with it'. The marriage was more important than the wedding, I said, and I hated the stupid matrimony plan-less limbo we'd arrived in. Wheels were soon set in motion: we'd invite only our immediate family and two witnesses to the ceremony, having a small evening party for everyone else. Setting aside the wedding scrapbook I'd been piecing together since I was nineteen, full of photographs of huge white weddings I'd snipped out of expensive bridal magazines, I grew comfortable with the idea of an 'intimate' celebration – it might have been a world away from the stately home and big dress I'd dreamed of (I bought my outfit and the flowers the day before from Monsoon Oxford Street and Columbia Road Flower Market respectively), but this was the way the celebrities did it, right?

With six weeks to go before the big day we still lacked the time (and inclination) to send out paper invites, so low-key Facebook event notifications were dispatched. The thirteen members of our wedding party expected at the ceremony received a phone call, and a round robin email was sent around our respective workplaces to let them know they'd be welcome at the free-for-all post-wedding party at a Farringdon nightclub.

On the day, our register office ceremony went by in a flash, with the technical term for my overriding emotion being 'shit scared'. There were tears from all in attendance and I was so overwhelmed by the entire day that my décolletage came up in angry red blotches, my chest predicting the outcome of my marriage more accurately than I could.

Amid confetti-laced beeps from traffic on the A40 we jumped in Ubers to take us to our reception lunch at the inevitable Shoreditch House, where we toasted our union with their cheapest house white in a private dining room we'd hired for half price (thank God for cheap Monday weddings). The lunch went by in a blur of chinking glasses and raucous laughter as we all necked lethal yet delicious espresso martinis in lieu of pudding.

Looking back, you'd be right to write us off as young and irresponsible from the off. How can a couple who can't be arsed to save up for their wedding day be expected to excel in marriage?

But we had optimism and youth on our side and a year and a half later we also had the surprise of our daughter's arrival, followed quickly by that of our son.

That morning in the grimy bedsit my role of dutiful wife and mother felt like a million miles away as I scurried around, searching for both my belongings and my dignity. With a soundtrack of mindless chatter directed at the man I'd woken up with – I still had no idea what his name was – I finally located those elusive knickers of mine.

Once my underwear had been firmly replaced on my body I locked myself in the cold loo, carefully placing the last scraps of the toilet roll on the cold seat as a barrier to the unsavoury germs lurking beneath. I sighed as I peed, my eyes roving over the mildewed shower, the rusty taps, the almost-empty bottles of bright blue Radox.

With the unmistakable furriness of last night's beer and burgers on my teeth, I longed to brush them; but the only toothbrush in the bathroom was perching on top of the cistern, and all I could think of was a newspaper article I'd read about the spread of faecal matter when you flushed. With my hangover settling in for the day I myself felt like faecal matter; the last thing I wanted to do was put someone else's in my mouth. I settled instead for a finger-ful of Colgate swished around my teeth.

I'd expected my first sexual encounter as a single woman to leave me feeling empowered, sexy, excited. Having been with only the father of my children for the last ten years, I'd been conditioned to believe all my single friends were having wild

swinging-chandelier sex. Their stories left me wide-eyed and
more than a little jealous, marvelling at the apparent in-the-sack
skills of their boyfriends, lovers and fuckbuddies.

In contrast, my sexuality had deserted me the moment I'd laid
eyes on a positive pregnancy test: once I'd learned that the direct
consequences of unprotected sex were pregnancy-related piles,
bulging varicose veins and all-day sickness it's no wonder I
ceased to feel like a sex kitten. And anyway, who wants their
nipples sensually caressed when there's a chance of them erupt-
ing with breast milk? I'm sure there are people out there for
whom that's their number-one sexual preference, but I certainly
wasn't one of them.

The one and only date I'd been on before meeting the man
who became my husband was with a boring postgrad physics
student from my university: we drank two-for-one cocktails at
the Pitcher and Piano and stumbled home to halls after a terrible
snog, an experience that was a million miles away from the fancy
dates of *Sex and the City* I felt I was owed. Meeting Will and
falling in love with him so young, I'd felt lucky to be exempting
myself from the terrible relationship experiences that my friends
were all going through, though nine years on as comfort turned
to complacency I was eager to get back out into the dating world,
eager to have some new experiences.

At the age of twenty-seven this new world of men, flirting,
nuance and innuendo had a funny effect on me. I felt like a caged
tiger, a dormant volcano, and though I was ready to rediscover
the way I vaguely remembered feeling when I first met Will, I was
also terrified of what might happen. I was desperate to live my
life by my hormones and the whims of my libido once more,

rather than having each day of my monotonous and repetitive life dictated to me by the family responsibility of two tiny people who couldn't even speak yet; but I also craved the security I had found in going to bed with the same man each and every night. I didn't know how to reconcile these two things into a life that would bring me eventual happiness.

As I sat on the cold toilet seat somewhere in north London all I could recall from the night before, my first groundbreaking and terrifying step into singledom, was a perfunctory shag, a 'wham, bam, thank you ma'am'-type encounter. It had felt robotic and automatic, with zero thought given to my needs or pleasure.

Why didn't the earth move? I wondered. Where were the fireworks to symbolise my independence from my marriage, my own private bed-based Fourth of July? They weren't to be found in the shameful pits of that London bedsit, that's for sure.

I wondered if my feelings of empowerment would come later, because all I felt that day was shame. Shame on me for getting drunk and going home with someone I wouldn't look twice at sober. Shame on me for having to face the Saturday morning train home in last night's knickers. Shame shame shame. I could have cried but I didn't: anything to get me on my way home as quickly as possible.

Not able to hide in the chilly bathroom any longer, I flushed the loo and, after a fruitless search for soap, washed my hands with the dregs of the blue Radox. Taking a deep breath, I faced my new acquaintance with more small talk, faking awkwardly bright conversation about the beer festival we'd been at, the tenuous mutual friends we barely had.

To end my own incessant nervous chatter I dressed quickly, finding my socks under his guitar, my camisole looped over his skateboard, my phone in the toe of my boot. Seemingly not caring that my teeth were dirty or last night's clothes were creased and beer-stained, he half-heartedly asked for my number before enquiring if I wanted him to walk me to the bus stop. Hoping he'd forget I ever existed, I gave him the wrong number, politely declined his escort to the bus stop and hurriedly made my escape.

Newington Green, a pleasant leafy area of London a little way north of Hoxton, was a haven compared to the oppressive flat I'd spent the last ten hours in. Though my mouth was fuzzy and my head just as much, I enjoyed the walk to the bus stop, processing the enormity of what had just happened.

The area was familiar, having been my home once upon a time, before motherhood. For a moment I slowed my pace and pretended this was still my neighbourhood, that I'd turn the corner and see my local pub, my old front door with my welcoming husband waiting behind the stacks of junk mail in the communal hallway. It felt comforting to think I could dig my keys out of my handbag and open the lock back into a life that was altogether way less complicated than the one I was currently living. I'd walk back into that big one-room space and flop on to the rented couch in the rented living room, thinking of nothing more than which takeaway I would order to sate my standard Saturday hangover.

Instead my thoughts turned back to my kids, my broken marriage and the day's responsibilities. Hangover be gone: I had to forget my inner turmoil and power home to take over childcare duties.

*   *   *

Walking through your front door when you've got small children waiting to greet you is one of the most special feelings on the planet. To them you are a celebrity, a hero . . . you may as well be made from chocolate, such is the excitement your sudden presence can prompt. The viral videos you watch on Facebook of men coming back from tours of duty to overexcited loving labradors? They're nothing in comparison to the frantic happiness of your kids when you've been away for twenty-four hours.

As they threw their arms around me I immediately thrust my nose into their downy heads, inhaling the scent that was undeniably them, a mix of sweetness and their lavender baby shampoo. Elfie at almost two was padding around in the pink pyjamas I'd bought her for Christmas that year, her light brown hair a bedhead mess that only small kids can get away with: her arms held tightly to my thigh as she cried 'MAMA!' Hux was still crawling; at only just a year old he followed Elfie with the empty feet of his grey onesie trailed behind him, a smear of Marmite over a gummy smile that displayed two bottom teeth. Will, my grim-faced ex-husband, followed closely behind.

At this point, the beginning of our split, Will and I didn't really speak, and when we did there was a certain lack of decorum. Despite our amicable separation there was still a huge amount of ill feeling on both sides: I felt short-changed that, even though he was 50 per cent responsible for the creation of our children he wasn't left with half of the responsibility for looking after them, citing work and commuting pressures as a reason to move from our Buckinghamshire home back to London. In turn, although our split was the right thing to do, I felt he blamed himself for moving away from his children, upset at the thought that it was necessary to be apart from them. Though ours had never been a volatile relationship before, now we took these feelings out on each other, resulting in a couple of arguments that could be kindly described as 'humdingers'.

I imagine few men enter into the decision to procreate lightly and I knew he'd always aspired to be the best dad possible. Although our separation was patently mutual I felt abandoned, felt he'd taken on the role of part-time parent all too quickly, and I was aggrieved that I couldn't move my life forward in the same way as him. He'd swiftly moved back to our old home area of east London to build a business and further his career, with the children spending only two weekends a month at his house, and I felt left behind, a dowdy suburban single mum with little hope of achieving the dreams I'd once had for myself.

Having found motherhood hard enough as part of a couple, I was terrified about how my life would pan out with a bi-weekend dad as the other parent in my equation. I felt stuck and suffocated in my situation. We'd happily relocated to Buckinghamshire as a family, but he'd left a single man while I picked up the pieces of our union. Plus I was deep in the thick of post-natal depression with a massive case of loneliness on the side – try getting out of the house to make friends at awkward baby groups when you can't even make it to the shower to wash your hair. I felt abandoned, left to sink in a sea of nappies, chapped nipples, resentment and limited child maintenance.

Before I'd had kids I felt like I'd been a person worth knowing. I worked for one of the biggest media brands in the world, managing a team of publishing professionals who all worked hard and partied harder. I spent days in meetings and evenings in restaurants, attended Fashion Week and spoke at conferences. I had the world at my fingertips.

And then I got pregnant.

I went from socialising in a domain of sycophants hanging on to my every word to taking care of a baby who only hung on to my cracked nipple. I no longer partied all night, but kept the same hours winding, changing nappies, feeding. I no longer worried about my shoes matching my dress, but became obsessed by the exact amounts my tiny offspring were eating, mithering over the colour and consistency of their stools with a fervency I'd previously only ever applied to who I'd be meeting backstage that weekend. My life was a monotonous cycle of activities that I got absolutely no thanks or recognition for: budgeting, bath-time, burping. Full of literal baby shit, it was foreign and boring . . . I felt like I'd gone from hero to zero in the space of a Caesarean section.

So when the divorce was decided upon I was at least a little thankful that I'd regain what I thought would be some independence. I knew I'd never regain my previous life of wanky media hobnobbing – the way my heart exponentially grew with childbirth put paid to ever being selfish again – but I was thrilled at the idea of all the fun and socialising I'd do. I'd get to drink interesting drinks with interesting people, go on my first date in ten years, actually see my friends in places that weren't our living rooms or the local Costa. It felt thrillingly fresh: to pinch the book title from my son Huxley's namesake, it was my very own brave new world.

Only that freshness was a long way away that Sunday as I dragged my hungover feet through my front door to be confronted with a fairly mute ex-husband and two children thrilled to be reunited with their mother. Lifting them into the air for a cuddle with my Radox-washed hands, I felt trashy and cheap, not liberated and independent as I had expected after my first (not-so) great sexual adventure.

I felt ashamed that I'd chosen a stranger's company over my children's, indulging my lust when I should have been at home reading them a bedtime story and tucking them in for the evening. I was a mum now: didn't that mean I shouldn't crave sex or passion? The whole point of parenthood was that you'd only ever have sex with the man who helped you create your children (and sometimes not even him). Now, separated, I felt like my genitals should have an impenetrable sheath over them, like a Barbie doll but a nun-type motherhood version, one who should be so busy concerning herself with her children's well-being that she ignored the call of her libido. Why would I be thinking about sex when I had my children to worry about?

This shame added an extra unwelcome layer to my hangover as I prepared my children's lunch in the kitchen I'd lovingly decorated with kitschy Cath Kidston touches only a couple of months before. Enlisting the help of my mother-in-law's sewing skills, I'd turned floral fabric into curtains and tablecloths, but now the bright and joyful flowery pattern of the signature print made a mockery of the last twenty-four hours, the children oblivious to my misery as they chatted baby nonsense to each other in their high chairs. My headache intensified as they banged their bright plastic spoons upon their bright plastic bowls.

I took a break from chopping cucumber and Cheddar into tiny palm-sized batons and leaned over the sink, gazing out to the garden where I'd planted spring bulbs in a therapeutic effort to make myself feel better about life and my marriage. I felt sick and wanted to heave, but instead I turned to the children and brightly presented them with the fruits of my lacklustre labours. If I'd learned anything about children in my two and a half years as a parent – and sometimes I felt like I really hadn't – it was that a lunch of cucumber and Mini Cheddars every so often wouldn't kill them.

I turned back to my sink safe haven. The shame now fitted well. I knew more of it was to come.

The man I'd chosen to make my first conquest, the guy who'd spent the previous night prodding my pants as if he was playing on a PlayStation, the one whose name still evaded me?

He hadn't worn a condom.

CHAPTER TWO

The Shame, Oh, The Shame

Child-wrangling with a hangover is a unifying experience. I imagine it happens the same way the world over: the pounding headache, the day-old gin or beer mouth, the aching eyes. The incredibly and unnecessary incessant LOUD NOISES from the people you created, the ones who on this day seem hell-bent on hurting you with their questions, their banging, their whining. I love my children as much as the next person, but when I'm nursing a head full of booze-induced pain and regret I *will* cry over the un-tuneful bashing of a wooden xylophone.

Whenever I am that hungover mother having to let her offspring happily ride her like a horsie I always think of the other parents going through exactly the same experience. It's a fact of life that whether in Milton Keynes or Marbella, on the odd occasions us parents forget we're unexciting responsible adults and knock back booze with the youthful recklessness of a nineteen-year-old it almost always ends in tears. Ours, our kids', and whomever's we moan to about our unrelenting hangovers.

The world over there were mothers whose stomachs undoubtedly churned with last night's excesses as mine did now, and that thought comforted me no end.

But comfort wasn't something I was feeling much of: though the bank holiday weekend shops were the last thing I wanted to tackle with my self-induced headache, I was off to find a pharmacy. And, because I was now a single mum, my kids would be coming with me.

At that point the morning-after pill was one of those abstract things I'd heard about in passing. It was a thing that girls who had crazy adventures with men they didn't know bought, not responsible mums like me who spent their lives with the same man, either pregnant or on the pill. Emergency contraception was something that happened on late night Channel 4 documentaries and Radio 1's *Newsbeat*, not in my house of sanctimony and virtue.

Not wanting what I was about to research to be traced by even my future self, I opened up an incognito browser on my laptop to search down the answers to the pressing questions I had about the morning-after pill. A quick google told me that I could get it from Boots, it'd cost me about twenty-five quid and the sooner I got it in me the better. Though I was agog at the price of it – I could have bought myself a couple of nice bottles of wine with that cash, though ironically it was about that much booze that had got me in this mess – I was somewhat comforted at one of the search engine's auto-complete options that presented itself: 'Morning-after pill twice in one week'. I might have been stupid but I vowed this would be the one and only time I'd make such a shameful pilgrimage to the pharmacy.

I left the remnants of the cheese and cucumber lunch on the kitchen table and strapped Elfie and Hux into their car seats ready for the twenty-minute ride into town. I was aggrieved, sure that in the cases of contraception mishaps I'd read about in *Glamour* magazine the chivalrous other half of the equation offered to pay for half the cost of the treatment: at that point I probably would have shoved twenty-five pounds in my own vagina to make sure a pregnancy didn't happen but I was sad that I didn't even know my guy's name, let alone feel able to ask him to PayPal me £12.50. Even with two babbling babies in the back of my car the thought made me feel lonely and upset; I turned the CD player on, thinking a rousing rendition of something by Mr Tumble would help lift the spirits, but nope, it just made my already-intense headache worse.

Reaching the shopping centre, I unloaded Elfie and Hux from the car, Hux's tiny hand stickily clasped in mine as I heaved him into the baby carrier. Pushing Elfie across the car park in her pushchair, I abstractly wondered how many seemingly responsible mothers of two had made just such a stride of shame to their local Boots. I hoped I wasn't the first but this wasn't exactly something I'd be bringing up with the married mums at next Thursday's sensory baby group.

The pharmacy counter was vast and busy. The queue snaked around the shop, almost reaching a display of eye care near the doors, and I pretended to study the contact lens solutions and eye baths while trying to covertly observe the chattering customers and staff. The last thing I wanted to do was bump into a relative or, even worse, a mum friend, so I skulked around quietly until I could be sure the coast was clear, then timidly joined the back of the queue. Elderly couples picking up their prescriptions looked on with smiles as I played peek-a-boo with Hux and mindlessly answered Elfie's questions, while I wished time would hurry the hell up so I could get back to the car and take myself home to the safe haven of my sofa.

I felt my face go hot as my point in the queue approached the counter.

'Next customer, please!' announced the pharmacy assistant, a woman who looked about my age.

I stepped forward. 'I need to speak to someone about the morning-after pill,' I all but whispered.

'The what?' she said, in a voice that sounded sixty decibels too loud. I cleared my throat and tried again.

'The morning-after pill, please.'

She looked at me with what I told myself was understanding but may well have been derision, and motioned for me to step aside. 'I'll get the pharmacist for you', she said.

In a move that at that moment could only be comically punishing, a wheel of the pram locked as I tried to move to the side of the counter: I stumbled and tripped over my feet, cradling Hux's head to keep it safe, turning bright red as the pram's wheels crashed noisily against the side of the counter.

'WHOOPSIDAISY!' Elfie announced, enjoying the overly wobbly buggy, grinning at the queue as she clapped her hands. Old ladies cooed back and I wanted to die. I grimaced a smile and hoped the ground would swallow me whole and transport me to a place where nobody ever required emergency contraception, even if that meant going to actual hell.

The middle-aged pharmacist approached, an efficient yet kindly look on her face. 'How can I help?' she asked, in a way that I hoped meant she dealt with much more embarrassing situations than this one on a daily basis. There was no point wishing a quick verruca or ingrown toenail on myself. I was going to have to tell this woman I had had sex with a stranger.

'I need the morning-after pill,' I said with a decisiveness I didn't feel.

She side-eyed my children and I could see her brain ticking over.

'Of course,' she said. 'I just need to ask you a couple of questions first.'

She asked me when I'd last had sex (ugh), whether I'd used any contraception (no, duh), when my last period was and whether I had any pre-existing conditions. She enquired about my health, my age, my medication. I felt naked, stripped of a shield that I'd been using to protect myself: standing at that pharmacy counter being questioned by a stranger with an MPharm degree brought up an inner vulnerability in myself that I hadn't felt in a long time.

I wanted to grab the woman in front of me and shake her, make her look me in the eye while I forcibly confirmed that *I am a good person*. I wanted to explain that I don't do this thing, this one-night-stand thing, that I have a family and a good moral compass. I wanted to outline the fact that although I loved the father of my children very much we just weren't *in love* any more, tell her that nobody could hate me any more for my marriage break-up than I did already and that I felt completely vile for sleeping with a stranger in some kind of misjudged quest to put my broken self back together again.

I wanted to ask for her help, not just for the morning-after pill but for the wisdom and grace to work out exactly what the hell I should do now that the man I had thought was going to be by my side for ever was sleeping in a house I'd never been to forty miles down the M1. I wanted to ask her how I could stop looking for comfort and answers in the wrong places.

But I didn't grab the pharmacist by the shoulders, as not getting arrested for assault was the one good thing this otherwise completely bleakly grey day had going for it. Contraception duly dispensed, I thanked her and left the counter with nothing more than a small packet of tablets

The ordeal had exhausted and broken me but I felt I must do something for my children to make up for unwittingly putting them through such a seedy experience, so decided that ice cream was the answer. Isn't ice cream always the answer?

Stopping only for me to swill back one of the two pills I'd been instructed to take with a glug of water, we grimly soldiered on to the ice cream shop. I brightly chattered to Elfie in her pram about the shopping centre's indoor palm trees and dinosaur displays, internally cringing as my tummy turned with hunger and shame.

At that moment I knew one thing for sure: after that experience I'd never feel embarrassed to ask a pharmacist for thrush cream again.

CHAPTER THREE

Brought Up By The Internet

I have always counted my mum as one of my best friends. We drive each other absolutely bonkers – I put this down to our personalities being too similar – but I wouldn't have it any other way. As tough women we're both headstrong, both powerful, both opinionated. We're outgoing, independent and sometimes, most annoyingly, can talk the hind legs off a donkey. If not to each other, then to – and over – other people.

We're not just similar in personality either: we look like the same person twenty-eight years apart, with the same brown hair, blue eyes and majestic (read: a bit too big) noses. My mum was always the one to arrive at parents' evenings and have the teachers give a knowing wink as they chuckled to her, 'I don't need to ask whose mother you are!'

For as long as I can remember I haven't gone twenty-four hours without speaking to my mum. Being so similar in not just looks but personalities, we usually have identical viewpoints; in my opinion there's nothing like having your outspoken beliefs justified in a too-long phone call to someone who thinks entirely the same as you, and that's what a chat with her always gives me. Satisfaction at its best, I reckon. I was one of those people who keenly felt the reproductive call of Mother Nature, and it was this brilliant relationship with my own mother that gave me the confidence to believe in and trust that I would also be a wonderful mum.

I believed my path to motherhood was clearly set for me as I'd seen in the movies and the chick-lit I loved to read: I'd do well at school, get into a good university, start a career and marry a lovely man before giving up work in pursuit of babies and baking. I'd do as my own mum had done and dedicate my life to ensuring my kids were loved and looked after to the fullest possible degree, living in a quiet village where I'd go from baby group to coffee shop to my kitchen and back again, cooking only with organic produce and mixing up the fluffiest cakes in a candy-coloured KitchenAid with my pigtail-toting toddler. My house would be immaculately decorated and I would host legendary five-course dinner parties twice a month to celebrate my hard-working husband, who would naturally be the most sparkling person at the table with me his slightly subservient sidekick. Our guests would go home not only talking in awe about the incredible food that was always served up at our flawless home, but also pondering what a loving and well-matched couple we were, wondering how my fictional husband and I got lucky enough to fall so deeply in love. And with such well-behaved children, too!

Thinking about my projected life plans now, I want to take a long nap.

My Hollywood vision of life hadn't accounted for the fact that I was a pretty stroppy and flighty teenager, invested more in having fun and seeing my friends than in A levels and university visits. Always eager to be an adult as soon as possible (if not sooner), I dropped out of sixth form, unceremoniously dumping my school bags and uniform in favour of a job as a trainee marketing executive at a local printing company. The office was manned by middle-aged women with names like Karen and Maureen, had green carpet tiles on the floor and smelled strongly of warm paper straight from a photocopier, but I had a desk of my own and could chirpily answer questions about paper on the phone to grown-ups who presumably believed I was the career-driven woman I had aspired to be. I'd finally arrived. This was it: Alice Judge-Talbot was a schoolkid no longer; she was a wage-earning professional, taking home the princely sum of £741 a month – a small fortune, enough to keep me in Topshop jeans for the foreseeable future.

It took approximately six weeks of me being that wage-earning professional before I realised that, though school was tough, work was infinitely tougher. And so I returned to school with my tail between my legs, uniform retrieved from the back of the wardrobe (my mum, knowing me as well as she did, had had the clever foresight not to let me *literally* dump it).

My last year of sixth form was difficult. Having had my dream life planned out for such a long time – the husband, the kids, the dinner parties – I couldn't see any kind of career longevity ahead and thought that by pursuing qualifications or a degree I'd be wasting my time. I was happy to coast until I met my hypothetical husband, certain that my innate desire to cherish both him and our imagined children would negate the need for any kind of job. I'd had vague thoughts of pursuing journalism, as I loved to write, and had applied for university courses in that vein, but having visited my local council's press office for work experience and been made to spend the entire time cutting stories out of a newspaper and sticking them in a scrapbook in the manner of an oversized toddler, I'd somewhat lost my passion for words. Yep, I knew for sure I'd be much better suited to a life of domesticity and stay-at-home motherhood.

And so I turned down the two university places I'd been offered to study journalism, one at the University of Lincoln and one at the University of Central Lancashire, deciding once again to stay at home and get a job instead, not even embarking on the brave trans-continent Gap Yahs that some of my peers were working towards.

But there was a reason my dad had spent my childhood calling me Little Miss Fickle and yep, you guessed it, I changed my mind again: in the summer when all my friends were preparing to leave home for their courses in Bristol, Cardiff and Leeds I decided I couldn't be left behind on my own. I wanted to go to university.

Fifteen years on and I can still remember the phone call I made to my mother to tell her I'd had a change of heart once more about higher education. It was a pouring wet day in July and I'd spent the previous couple of weeks with friends who were preparing for their further educational departures to exciting and grown-up-sounding cities all over the country. All of us were nearing the seminal age of eighteen, spending our social time frequenting our local town's boozers in uniforms of jeans and a nice top (they had to be Oasis, Kookaï or Warehouse, natch) with our fake IDs clutched tightly in our sweaty palms. We'd excitedly discuss what life outside our small Worcestershire town might bring us in the next few years as we got tipsy on Malibu and Archers before our parents picked us up for our 11 p.m. curfews.

Except me: I was the only one who knew exactly where I'd be for the foreseeable while my friends were all living on their own in their new city's halls of residence or university flats. I'd be at home with my mum, dad and brother, the same place I'd been for the first eighteen years of my life, living my days not with an exciting group of new friends in an exciting new city but with my sixteen-year-old brother sleeping underneath posters of Buffy the Vampire Slayer in the bedroom next to mine.

At the same time as I was necking overly sweet drinks in the local Wetherspoons I was living something of a double life: one real, one virtual. With a technologically forward dad as my hero – in the 90s he had a car phone, an actual breezeblock-sized car phone – our family were early adopters of the internet. It arrived in our home in 1999, a massive 56k modem that sat atop our bulky desktop computer and changed our lives for ever. Living as I did in a tiny village that lacked even a shop, that modem was my route to the glamour of the outside world. It gave me a life outside of Pony Club and the back-seat politics of the school bus. The first time I logged on I was hooked, that screechy scratchy static sound of the connection signalling the commencement of my social life.

As a bored fourteen-year-old I connected to people all over the world via Yahoo! Chat Rooms and typed missives to my school friends nightly on MSN Messenger. Even now seeing the clock click over from 5.59 to 6 p.m. gives me a slight thrill: that time always signalled the beginning of our home phone's off-peak tariff, meaning I could begin my nightly hour on the web for 1p a minute rather than the Mum-anointed 'extortionate' 3p. I'd log on for my allotted hour and delight in the new world I was discovering, disconnecting only if Mum wanted to use the phone.

Our old noisy modem also brought to me the platform LiveJournal, an online diary where users could connect with 'friends' and grant them access to read their innermost thoughts. As a teenager with more feelings and emotions than I knew what to do with – between the ages of fourteen and seventeen I'd often spend hours wailing in the style of a hormonal banshee on my bathroom floor for no other reason than 'life wasn't fair' and 'I didn't ask to be born' – this safe space became a wonderfully therapeutic outlet. In it I documented my stories of family, friends, boys, boys and boys:

I had eye contact with Mark today on the science block stairs, it was electric!! He slowly walked past me and I could smell his aftershave, I think it was Calvin Klein. He has the bluest blue eyes and such lovely blond hair. We definitely have a connection, I think I'll say hello to him next time: he might know who I am now, OMG!! My friend Philippa says she'll ask him if he wants a girlfriend!

Repeat ad infinitum.

Sometimes I miss the simplicity of those relationships I had when I was younger. Like the one I enjoyed with Mark Watson, a boy two years above me in school. I thought he was dreamily perfect; tall and lanky with a blue Eastpak bag – I bought a baby pink one to match as soon as I had the pocket money. I didn't speak to him once in the three years we were at the same school, yet in my head (and on my LiveJournal) I was utterly in love. He added me on Facebook ten years later and the friend request gave me butter-flies that took me right back to 1999. Even now I can't say his name without hearing some quality of reverent awe in my voice.

Matt never knew we were in an imagined relationship but I spent hours, absolutely hours, daydreaming about the life we'd have together. Imagining him in a suit and a tie as he trotted off to work in the morning with a belly full of the breakfast I'd made him in the cottage we shared with our two blonde chil-dren, making him lavish dinners ready for his return to our country kitchen . . . I'd planned out the perfect life for him and yet he didn't know I even existed.

Then there was the internet boyfriend I had for three months at some point in my fifteenth year. We met in a Yahoo! Chat Room: his name was Brant, he was two years older than me, ergo impossibly sophisticated and mature, and he lived a comforting 5,000 miles away in Texas. My relationship with Brant meant I had all the benefits of boasting to my friends about having a boyfriend, yet I didn't have to worry about any of the terrifying accoutrements – hand-holding, snogging, the anticipation of sex – that came with it. Plus, hormonal teen-agers that we were, we were both into the emo genre of music: he'd send me mix CDs of music he thought I'd like, my favourite songs having uplifting titles such as 'At Your Funeral', 'The Calendar Hung Itself' and 'If I Told You This Was Killing Me, Would You Stop'? Teenage angst . . . we revelled in it.

I'd recommend an internet boyfriend to anyone. Totally non-threatening, it really cuts out the hassle of interacting with an actual person, as long as you don't end up on *Catfish* because the object of your romance is in fact a middle-aged stained-vest-wearing pervert called Malcolm living in his mum's house. Plus the online relationship is great for your future career prospects: I learned how to touch-type in my hours writing long and involved emails to Brant alongside pounding away at my online diary. My 65 WPM typing speed stood me in very good stead when I was looking for my first temp jobs – thanks, internet.

I have Brant and my globe-wide LiveJournal pals – Daile in America, Jill in Australia, even Gemma in London – to thank for my changing my mind about university. Yes, my friends at home would bang on about the new halls of residence they'd be moving into all over the country and make me feel a slight longing for what might be, but it was my internet pals who taught me there might just be life outside of the ten-mile radius I'd grown up in. Their lives seemed exotic, fun and interesting; the most excitement we had in provincial-town, Worcestershire, was a PA at the local sticky-floored nightclub from the week's *Big Brother* reject.

So it was that wet day in July right around my eighteenth birthday when I made the decision to go to university. I'd picked up my A level results a couple of days previously in my little Fiat Cinquecento, the car my parents had bought me for my seventeenth birthday. My results weren't bad (though would have been better if I'd spent less time skiving off for trips to Topshop), but the overconfident, naive eighteen-year-old me knew that if I wanted to go to university hard enough I would bloody do it, good A levels be damned.

Still having vague aspirations of writing in some way, shape or form, I looked into doing an English literature course. But of course these degrees were all oversubscribed by people who actually worked hard at their A levels, people who'd spent the last two years striving towards their higher-educational goals rather than the last two minutes like me. In the end, clutching the phone in one hand and a crumpled copy of *The Times*'s clearing listings in the other, I started combing through the available spaces at the University of Nottingham, a campus uni I'd visited only a year before with my best friend: her brother was in his third year and we'd taken the opportunity to drive up the motorway and live the proper student life for a weekend (sleeping on sofas, 99p cocktails, Super Noodles: done).

There was one course that fitted my loose requirements (i.e. there were spaces available and my results would grant me entry) but I'd never heard of it previously: a sociology and social policy BA degree. Apparently a little sister to sociology, it explored social problems and welfare issues through social theories and research, ironically something the present-day Labour-voting single-parent me would take a huge interest in, although at the age of eighteen with a very cushy middle-class upbringing, I wouldn't have known the definition of white social privilege if it socked me in the face with a fish. But when faced with the exciting prospect of going to university that small detail didn't worry me. Moving to a city, doing the impossibly grown-up sounding thing of 'going to lectures', was the name of the game and I didn't care much what I'd study: I couldn't have chosen to learn about something more foreign, yet if it would get me out of my hometown and towards something bigger I was in.

31

My parents, God love them, took my new change of heart in their stride and four weeks later were driving me up the M1 to my slightly whiffy student flat on the outskirts of Nottingham.

NOW I had arrived. I was finally, after a few false starts, a grown-up. And I couldn't wait for my life to begin.

CHAPTER FOUR

Becoming A Mother When The Only One You Know Is Your Own

I find out I'm pregnant in November. I'm off work with suspected swine flu, a disease that is doing the rounds on the news and is therefore worthy of a couple of sick days, and though I've probably just got a bad cold I've dragged myself to the pharmacy to pick up Tamiflu because NHS Direct has told me I have to. I'm tired and feel weirdly sick but put it down to the lurgy and try to enjoy a couple of days away from the office.

We weren't trying to have a baby, not really. I'd spent my later teenage years crippled once a month by endometriosis, a condition that – pleasantly – means your endometrial lining (the stuff that grows and sheds once a month on the inside of your uterus) appears in other parts of your body: during keyhole surgery at age nineteen mine had been lasered off my urethra, bowel and ovaries, a procedure that was about as pleasant as it sounds. Knowing I'd like to have children in the future, one of the questions I'd asked my gynaecologist on coming round was how the condition would affect my fertility.

He sat down on my bed, patting the hand that didn't have a cannula sticking out of it:

'I wouldn't hang around if you want to have children,' he said.

I took this to mean Will and I would be fairly screwed – literally and figuratively – when it came to conceiving, so after we were married I came off the pill or, as one friend tastefully put it, 'removed the goalie' and bought a copy of the classic tome *Taking Charge of your Fertility*. As I rationalised to Will, it would be a nightmare if we'd tried to get pregnant in five years' time, only to find out we were barren and have to go to the end of the IVF waiting lists. Better to just give it a test now so we could queue for treatment as soon as we were ready to have a family.

I didn't even get past the introduction of my fertility book: one month later I was pregnant.

In anticipation of learning more about my fertility I'd bought a job lot of basal temperature monitors, ovulation indicators and pregnancy tests off eBay so I was well-prepared for this moment, if only practically rather than emotionally. On my swine-flu-sanctioned fourth day of absence from work I had realised that my period seemed to be a couple of days late, and out of extreme boredom and email avoidance I decided to take one of said tests. Not really expecting anything other than that it would be an interesting way to fill ten minutes, I peed in a glass in our rented loo in north London, dipping one of my flimsy eBay sticks in.

Two lines appeared immediately, so I repeated the process once more. And again. And yeah, maybe one final time after that. I couldn't believe my eyes.

In a panic I called my husband at work, sputtering something incomprehensible that ended in me saying, 'COME HOME

NOW.' Always the workaholic, Will had never left work early for anything in his life but something in my voice that day convinced him. He appeared at the door of our flat a long thirty minutes later, asking with worried eyes if I was OK.

'I think I'm pregnant,' I stammered.

'You think?' he said.

'You tell me,' I replied, thrusting a handful of urine-soaked sticks under his nose. 'Do these look like lines to you?'

'I think you're pregnant,' he affirmed.

We looked at each other in disbelief, not knowing what to do or say.

'I'm pregnant,' I repeated. 'Holy fuck.'

I was twenty-four and didn't know any pregnant people or parents, so aside from taking a pregnancy test I wasn't sure what the process was. I knew you had to see a midwife at some point but how? And where?

I googled 'I think I'm pregnant' and followed the advice I found to book an appointment with my doctor, managing to get one allocated to me that evening.

Will and I left the house ten minutes before we were due at the surgery for the chilly walk down Kingsland Road to the GP, me clutching my bouquet of pregnancy tests carefully cosseted in a sandwich bag. These tests were duly displayed to the GP: 'Congratulations!' he exclaimed, before a worried frown crossed his brow. 'This is a congratulations-type situation, isn't it?' he said to check.

We both nodded in shock and he referred us to the midwifery team, an appointment that would be an agonisingly long six weeks away. Shell-shocked yet excited, we walked home via the newsagent, spending a tenner on extortionately priced baby magazines.

That evening, at a loss with what to do with myself, I opened up my work laptop and started typing. I'd met Will at eighteen and my use of my confessional LiveJournal had tapered off with my unrequited loves, but at this point finding an outlet for my worry and general state of early-pregnancy freaked-out-ness seemed like a necessity. So I started an anonymous blog, calling it Womb With A View: a knee-jerk reaction to the news I'd never expected to hear.

Through my new online space I found a whole network of women just like me, ones who had all these thoughts and feelings, questions and worries about pregnancy and babies. With no bump to speak of and a whole host of freaky symptoms – I only wanted to eat potato waffles with vinegar and had nightly baths because I, weirdly, enjoyed chewing wet flannels – my blog was an absolutely crucial outlet.

We found out we were expecting a girl about sixteen weeks in, fairly early on in the process. With that drawer full of pregnancy tests weighing heavy on my mind, I'd been taking one every week or so. In some way I enjoyed seeing that line constantly appear on the strip, giving me the reassurance that there actually was a baby inside me: with no external symptoms other than slightly sore boobs and no period, I needed the additional nod that I wasn't going mad, there was going to be a baby. But at around fifteen weeks the lines on my trusty sticks started getting lighter, and so I made another emergency appointment to see my doctor with another sandwich bag full of pee sticks. Taking pity on the panic from a lady who was at the least very hormonal, the doctor booked me a scan at the early pregnancy unit to set my mind at ease. The baby was totally healthy – bouncing around on the inside of my uterus, in fact – and I was made to promise not to take any more pregnancy tests. And she was a girl!

I was delighted – I'd always envisaged a mini-me growing inside my expanding belly – and from the moment I knew our It was a She I was in love. Elfreda Daphne was to be her name, the names of my grandmother and Will's, and we'd call her Elfie.

My pregnancy was fairly uneventful but that didn't mean it was easy. I suffered with incredible nausea throughout, quelled only by lying down and going to sleep. I was never sick but constantly felt on the brink of a heave or throw-up the entire time bar approximately four weeks, making tube and bus journeys interesting to say the least. This meant I could barely stand to eat at the beginning (cue lots of 'Wow, you look amazing! Have you lost weight?' comments from friends and acquaintances who had no idea I was With Child) and when I could face putting things near my mouth it was bland food only – toast, breadsticks, plain jacket potatoes. I piled Trump levels of fake tan on because it was the only thing that made me feel human, although in reality I ended up just looking shades of citrus.

I loved nothing more than to spend my evenings on the sofa or in the bath (preferably the bath because it meant I'd get to chew on those flannels), watching our little alien baby inside me. Though I was still majorly freaked out, it was the most fascinating of experiences; you feel everything from the stretches to the hiccups and the kicks and I couldn't get over the mind-blowing fact that I was growing a person *from scratch* inside me. Elfie was in the breech position and, with her head uncomfortably wedged somewhere near my ribs, I'd spend my days at work stroking her head and down her spine through my stomach, marvelling at the miracle that was going on inside me. It felt like a gross and nauseating miracle, sure, but a miracle all the same.

Though what was going on inside my belly happened like clockwork, the outside world was proving a little more tumultuous for our little family. Halfway through my pregnancy my father-in-law fell very ill with cancer, so Will jetted off to where his parents lived in Greece for a week to support both his father and his mother. Sadly the cancer proved to be terminal and he passed away only weeks later, with the family understandably devastated. My thirty-week bump accompanied me over to the little Greek island for the funeral and a very sad goodbye.

Only days after returning to England we were dealt another blow: Will was made redundant. With my salary soon to become statutory maternity allowance and no real job prospects on the horizon for him (dance music promotion being somewhat of a niche career choice), we made the decision to move back to Nottingham, to the house we'd bought four years previously before renting it out for our move to London.

With our lives in such a state of flux and with no concrete reason to stay in the capital, I imagined it would feel comforting for us to return to such familiarity; the place we'd met and fallen in love, the town that housed so many of our best friends. I didn't count on it feeling like such a step backwards, yet at the same time into the unknown.

Looking back, this was our first shift into parenthood and its accompanying anonymity, the morph from individuals to Mum and Dad, from immaturity to responsibility. When we lived in London we were known, we had jobs, careers, reputations. If we wanted something – a restaurant reservation, tickets to a festival, a connection – we emailed someone and got it. Back in Nottingham we were just another couple in a suburban home living a suburban life. I missed my friends and I missed feeling like a big fish in our little east London pond.

Elfie remained steadfastly breech for the entirety of the pregnancy, an impressive display of stubbornness that has translated through to her childhood. Knowing that if this didn't change I'd be facing a Caesarean section (and feeling frustrated at the time I'd spent learning all about hypnobirthing), I did everything I could to try to turn her: maniacally bouncing up and down on my yoga ball, climbing up the stairs on all fours. At thirty-seven weeks pregnant I even tried acupuncture as a last resort, having read online (where else?) that it was a fail-safe way to turn a breech baby. That ended in embarrassment: midway through my 10 a.m. appointment I fainted, coming round only for the practitioner to try to sell me a litany of Chinese herbs to correct the apparent chi imbalance that had led me to pass out. I left with his advice ringing in my ears – to eat more than a banana for breakfast when pregnant (you try eating more than a banana when your guts are constantly trying to eject themselves from your body, mate) – and went home to sit in bed, drink a cup of tea and eat a packet of Smarties. Looking at my piles of hypnobirthing books on my bedside table, I was gutted. I'd never pictured myself having a C-section and, despite not having the highest pain threshold ever, I'd been determined to bloody breathe and push this baby out.

Elfie was a footling breech, meaning one of her legs was dangling dangerously close to my cervix. It sounded very comfy to me, but had I gone into labour naturally it could have ended in disaster: as the feet are so much smaller than the head it would have put her at risk of slipping feet-first through a partially opened cervix before the rest of her body was ready to be born. Putting my disappointment over my lack of vaginal birth aside, I felt special that this super-rare type of birth presentation had chosen us, not knowing it was only the tip of the iceberg.

Elfie was born by Caesarean section on a Wednesday, 7 July 2010, a whole week before her due date. True to form, I'd covered myself in fake tan the night before (wanting to make a good impression on the hospital nurses and visitors' cameras, you understand), and though I can't remember the song she was born to I do remember Katy Perry and Snoop Dogg's 'California Gurls' being number one that week. What a jam, eh?

In the photos snapped by Will and the theatre staff I look fazed, drugged-up, happy: in one of them a tear sneaks out of the corner of my eye as I twist my head while still open and covered up on the operating table; in another I'm gazing down at my new baby in wonder and awe.

I so wish I could recall more of that day, the day that made me a mother. No doubt if I did it again now it'd be Instagram-storied and recorded to within an inch of its life and I almost wish it was – back then I was so bamboozled by the fact that I was giving birth that most of those memories have been relegated to an inaccessible place in my temporal lobe.

At the young age of twenty-four, becoming a mum was such a foreign concept to me; despite spending nine months growing a baby inside my uterus I can see now that I never got my head around it: I was still a child myself, I wasn't ready to birth another. I hadn't been able to cope with having a pet dog, had never successfully kept a plant alive and hated everything poo- and sick-related, so how was I expected to look after an actual human baby?

As my abdomen was stapled back together and I was propped up in recovery a kind nurse aided me to shove my nipple towards my baby. Having never as much as sunbathed topless before, I found this manhandling of my mammaries totally foreign and weird, but of course I did what I was told and Elfie duly suckled on my exposed breast. I looked at my lumpy naked body and back to her in shock and awe: I was a mum.

CHAPTER FIVE

The Nightmare of Motherhood

The thing I remember most vividly about my daughter being born is just how gross the whole experience was. As a feminist I'm constantly and consistently impressed by the absolutely incredible physical feats we women achieve on the daily – but let's face it, the whole gestation and birth situation is probably the least dignified experience one can go through. I blame Hollywood for the sterile version of childbirth we're provided with: even the movie I'd regard as most closely resembling gestation and birth, *Knocked Up*, uses altogether non-accurate depictions of birth (save perhaps for the 'crowning' shot – I defy anyone to watch this without crossing their legs).

In hindsight I was thankful for my enforced Caesarean: I might not have birthed my baby on a lily pad, as was my wish, in a chilled-out hospital pool with candles and aromatherapy, but my very medicalised sunroof birth experience was actually great. As a control freak I took great pleasure in the fact that I knew when it would be happening and could go to bed the night before having physically and mentally prepared myself for having a baby the next day. My hospital bag was packed with carefully washed and folded babygrows, the co-sleeping cot was erected and ready next to my side of the bed and an empty car seat sat waiting expectantly in the back of our new-to-us Renault Laguna. The only thing I had no control over was the time the birth would be, though having what I knew to be an unusual (and dangerous) breech presentation, I knew I'd be whipped in pretty sharpish.

We arrive on the ward on the warmest day of the year thus far at 7.00 a.m., a time that, as a committed night owl and late riser, I would usually only see if I'd stayed up too late the night before, but which, as I'm constantly told by chortling strangers, will become my new normal. I roll my eyes at them, thinking to myself how this baby will fit around my schedule, not me around hers. Seven years on I roll my eyes again at the naivety I nurtured about having children who would a) sleep and b) do what they're told. Ah, the optimism of a first-time mum!

The hospital is too warm and feels sticky, even at this early hour. The nerves set in as I'm shown to a bed on a ward with three other women who are either in the early stages of labour or have just given birth, and I distract myself by strapping on compression stockings (sexy) and larking about in my backless gown (ditto).

I feel as big as a house and look not unlike one in my billowing blue NHS attire: before leaving the house for the post-natal ward I weighed myself and discovered that I weighed in at 11 stone 11 pounds, having started my pregnancy journey at 9 stone 2. My fingers are so swollen that I can't slide my wedding and engagement rings on, so they're on a chain round my neck, my bump is tight and insanely itchy and my ankles so large I seem to have lost my ankle bones. I had never experienced acid reflux before I reached the latter stages of pregnancy and I am thoroughly sick of sleeping sitting up with a bottle of Gaviscon to hand, painful Braxton Hicks contractions have plagued me for the last two months, I waddle instead of walk and have piles – yep, PILES, at the age of twenty-four. I am so more than ready to give birth to this baby, though the less I think about her actual exit from my body the better.

I finally get walked down to the operating theatre at midday and this is the first time I completely understand the purpose of nil by mouth. I'm mad with nerves but even madder with hunger and I deduce that not being able to eat before an operation is not about negating the risk of food from the stomach being aspirated into the lungs and more about driving patients round the bend with hunger so they cease to worry about whichever operation they're about to go through.

My anaesthetist is a lovely man in his sixties who, as I am walked into theatre and climb up a weird kind of stepladder onto a high operating table, gently speaks to me about his daughter who's recently had a baby. It's all quite freaky-feeling, being awake and alert in an operating theatre.

'Why are they called theatres?' I wonder out loud to my assembled audience of doctors, midwives and assistants. 'It doesn't look like anyone's ever given an Olivier-winning performance in here.'

They all chuckle because hey, I'm the person about to get sliced open on the operating table so they have to, and continue

45

to bustle about with their officious-looking medical tasks. Feeling a bit disappointed that the operating room is more *Holby City* than *Grey's Anatomy*, I start to take an interest in the tasks that are going on around me.

As I'm the biggest fan of Google around (and have already been on maternity leave for a boring three weeks), I have obviously researched to death the process that a person goes through when given a spinal block like mine: the procedure sounds scary, precise and dangerous. I suddenly start panicking about what my anaesthetist is up to, pondering my fears. A rogue needle to the spine, perhaps, a slip that'll cost me the mobility in my legs or a lot of pain that I really don't fancy? It's amazing to think how much trust I've put in this kindly stranger who I've never met before, and I chatter inane crap at him, asking what he's doing, enquiring sixteen times whether or not he's remembered to do my local anaesthetic first as I read on Dr Google. He humours me and I'm impressed at his ability to chat back without barking at me to 'Sit still and be quiet', as I probably would if it were my job to come at a heavily pregnant woman's spine with a massive needle. Anaesthetic administered and certified – nope, I definitely can't feel a thing – I'm laid down on the table and covered in iodine.

I've always been on the prudish side about being naked, so I'm surprised at my devil-may-care attitude to the current situation: there I am, beached-whale-sized, reclining on a sterile bed, not able to feel or move the majority of my body. My gown has been folded up to expose my naked bottom half, with only my over-sized breasts covered by a blue sheet. My massive protruding bump hides my feet and the rest of my naked body, but I can still see medical professionals pottering around me.

Before long a screen is erected so all I can see is blueness, and my husband appears at my head. We've been talking for months about the excitement of him getting 'scrubbed in' to watch his daughter being born, though now, in his surgical cap and gown, he looks unsure and nervous.

The procedure begins and I'm surprised at the amount of small talk happening over my baby protrusion while the work on my abdomen goes on. It's not long before the midwife asks if Will would like to watch his daughter being born, so he leans forward over my protective screen. I swiftly ask him to move back: I can see the reflection of my wide-open abdomen in his glasses and it's freaking me out almost past the point of comfort. I may have come to terms with having a Caesarean but I don't want to actually *see* it.

I remember being mostly surprised (and disgusted) by the vernix that was all over Elfie when she was lifted victoriously, *Lion King*-style, up out of my cavernous belly. A white and greasy substance that covers a baby while they're in the womb, vernix develops on the skin at around twenty-seven weeks gestation, protecting the baby from amniotic fluid and any germs inside and outside the womb. Natural birth enthusiasts urge that this stuff be rubbed into the baby as soon as it enters the world (vernix, a substance unique to humans, is also a skin cleanser and antioxidant, fact fans), but I was totally unprepared for my baby, the one I thought would be a clean English-rose-coloured mewling bundle, to be thrust towards me covered in the stuff.

On her entrance into the world at 1.35 p.m. Elfie was wrapped in a towel and swiftly given to me – at least as much as that was physically possible when I was sliced from hip to hip and numb from the chest down. This bundle of baby held close to my nose was an excellent distraction from what was going on south of the screen that had been erected: when they tell you that a C-section feels like 'washing up inside your abdomen' it seems they are not wrong; there are all sorts of tugs and pulls going on that you can almost-but-not-quite feel. It's an incredibly unusual experience, not one I would rush to go through again.

As I looked at the face of this baby it felt incredibly foreign. I wasn't sure if I knew what was supposed to happen to me on ejecting a child from my body: I'd read mothers' anecdotes about lightning moments of recognition, huge realisations of love, moments of instant clarity. But all I felt was a slight confusion and panic at the new human that had appeared from what felt like nowhere, the tiny being with an elephant-sized presence that all the medical professionals were fussing over. I smiled because I believed that's what I was expected to do, a single tear escaping down the side of my face helped by gravity; I was unsure if its source was happiness or panic. I found it impossible to marry together the fact that I was pregnant a moment ago but now there was a baby, and that baby was mine and had come from me. I had produced a whole entire human, a little 6lbs 14oz life.

According to my midwife, babies are usually ejected with a little less of the aforementioned vernix than Elfie, but as my daughter was delivered early she was pretty damn covered in the stuff. I almost recoiled from its waxy sensation as I moved my head forward to kiss her perfect little button nose. She didn't scream like a Hollywood baby but instead gazed around with her intense dark eyes, looking like she was drinking in the new world around her. She was then dressed in a comically large terrycloth nappy and handed to her dad so my abdomen could be repaired. Fifteen staples scarily close to my vagina later – they all went in with what sounded like the same staple gun as a primary school teacher would use to make jaunty Easter wall displays – I was wheeled through to recovery.

I believe one of the biggest tragedies of our childbearing times is that we're not briefed on how difficult breastfeeding can be. When we first become mothers we're told that breast is best. We're supplied with leaflets depicting happy and well-rested mothers nursing their children, smiles and strategically placed sunbeams on their faces as they are coached by midwives on nipple placement and the rugby ball technique. I wanted desperately to breastfeed because I knew how good it was going to be for my new baby, how naturally it would come to me, how much easier it would be on my wallet. I knew it was best not only for Elfie but for me too: with nipple stimulation my uterus would contract, I'd burn the baby weight faster, I'd sleep better. For me there was no other option.

Until I actually did it and understood just how painful it could be. Where was the leaflet featuring the woman with a tear-stained face, attempting to clamp a screaming, hungry baby to her red-raw, bleeding breast?

My Caesarean section wasn't anything like the pain of breast-feeding. In comparison the operation to remove Elfie from my body had been carried out not by scalpel-wielding surgeons but by gentle kittens licking my abdomen: when feeling I was in so much pain I likened my baby trying to sustain herself at my breast to pulling barbed wire out of my nipples. I physically felt sick when I thought about feeding time, dragging myself to the sofa with a bottle of moisturising Lansinoh, bloodstained pads in my bra and a heavy heart. The latch caused my stomach to heave as my toes literally curled at the excruciating pain of my baby suckling at my nipple, as I wondered how something that was sold as being so natural could be the most hideous thing I'd ever felt in my life.

Breastfeeding aside, being the mum of a newborn was really hard, a world away from my expectation, and I was surprised that I didn't take to it as I thought I would. Having believed so much of motherhood would come to me as instinct, I'm shocked in its early stages at how much time I spend on Google, asking questions about sleep, eating, poo and those weird belly-button-stump things. I am in a lot of pain from my C-section incision, which compounds my tiredness, and Elfie has a lot of trouble eating, another layer of worry to slap on over my new-baby paranoia. I mix the breastfeeding with bottles of formula to try to give my breasts relief from the inescapable pain of feeding – and so begins my first experience of motherhood guilt: she is sick more than I'd like, although at the first of many doctor's visits I'm told this is completely normal in all new babies (spoiler: it isn't).

I continue to be overwhelmed at the way my body is healing and behaving. Although my stomach has contracted almost back to its normal size (long live the snap-back features of a body in its mid-twenties!), my boobs have taken on lives of their own and often propel milk out at the funniest times; in the shower, when getting changed, on one memorable occasion while I'm looking at trainers in Office. There are lumps and bumps where there were none before, most notably a prominent mum-tum and a bulging varicose vein at the back of my right knee; looking at this new, foreign body of mine, not to mention how much of it I'm giving to my baby, I feel a bit lost. I don't own myself any more; I'm owned by my child.

Elfie is not a happy baby. She cries a lot, does not sleep well and is starting to develop symptoms suggesting that all is not right – the skin on her head, which was at first prone to slight cradle cap, now flakes off in huge scary chunks. Her weight, which has always been less than it should be, keeps going down rather than up, each cross on the weight chart in her baby book a marker that somehow, in some way, I am failing here. My local health centre cancels weigh-in clinics for a month, so we aren't seen for a while, and she puts on only a tiny 6oz in this time, her body all ribs and jutting knees, her big eyes looking hugely forlorn in a face that's lacking baby chub. I see my own doctor, I see a locum doctor, I see a nurse: medical professionals at my local surgery, who all make me feel like a neurotic new mother and send me away.

It takes my mother convincing me to take Elfie along to her local doctor's surgery in Milton Keynes, and a concerned health visitor there, to really get me worried about my little girl's health. Looking her over, the health visitor is kind and gentle to me, sensing my absolute heart-sinking and hand-wringing helplessness at the fact that my baby won't eat, keeps vomiting, won't put on weight. She doesn't have the usual chubby, dimpled knees of a two-month-old but, instead, bony chicken legs, and her ribs protrude where we should see a fat happy Father Christmas belly. The health visitor tells me to feed her every three hours like clockwork.

Google gives me no answers. My GP has, once more, told me absolutely nothing is wrong. I feel utterly useless as a parent and human being, no longer trusting the instincts that are shouting at me that something is wrong, something is desperately wrong.

Two weeks later, in a last-ditch attempt to make my baby happy I stage something of a sit-in at my GP's surgery, refusing to leave until he refers me to the paediatric clinic at the Queen's Medical Centre in Nottingham. They agree she seems poorly and take blood to check whatever it is medical professionals check in these situations.

On my drive home I receive a phone call. An authoritative voice on the other end of the line tells me not to panic, so of course I immediately start to panic. 'Drive home carefully,' it says. 'Pack two bags, one for you, one for your baby. Don't rush yourself, but please get back to the hospital as soon as you can.'

I return to the hospital, laden like a packhorse with the accoutrements of babyhood: bottles, onesies, blankets, muslins. On arriving at the children's ward I'm given the devastating news that something is desperately, nearly deathly, wrong. They're unsure exactly what the problem is but they do give me the devastating news that, with Elfie's dangerously low sodium and high potassium levels that have gone untreated, my baby is mere days away from death. I'm told that it's only my perseverance and sheer bloody-mindedness, along with the hours spent forcefully trying to load my baby up with milk, that mean she is still alive today, that she hasn't experienced fits, that she's not brain-damaged.

The doctors don't know the extent of Elfie's ill health for a few days. She's a teeny-tiny pincushion, having blood taken from every available space on her little body; at one point they run out of test sites so begin drawing blood from her ankles. She's given an IV to stabilise her salt and potassium levels and we're warned that this medical thing, the one nobody can decipher just yet, will nonetheless mean she'll be on medication for the rest of her life.

I don't cry. I am numb. Will and I joke around with medical gloves and cardboard vomit bowls, wanting to do anything but accept the reality of our situation. I cuddle my tiny daughter with her huge splinted and bandaged arm, cringing each time yet more blood is taken from her or she's loaded up with further invasive drugs. I have to leave the room as a feeding tube is forced into her nose, as I can't stand to watch the sterile hands that pin her down while she gags.

After two days in hospital we're told to brace ourselves: Elfie's problem affects her sex hormones and the doctors are unsure what gender she actually is. Will and I look at each other and can only laugh at the ridiculousness of our situation, and the completely bonkers news we've just been given. 'How on earth will I announce on Facebook that she's actually a boy?!' I wonder out loud when I can take a breath through my hysterical and slightly crazy laughter.

Driving home for a shower and a sleep that afternoon is when the enormity of the situation finally hits me. I'm mindlessly listening to Radio 1, tapping my fingers on the steering wheel, thinking of absolutely nothing because, after two days of not sleeping on a camp bed next to my baby's hospital cot, I can't face my own thoughts. Bruno Mars comes on the radio, crooning 'Just The Way You Are', and I listen to the lyrics:

When I see your face, there's not a thing that I would change, cos you're amazing, just the way you are.

I can't stop seeing Elfie's face, the beautiful face of my baby girl, lying in hospital with tubes and wires snaking out of her. I don't know how to process what's happening to her so I break down and cry all the way home. I cry driving past commuters at the tram stop, I cry driving along the Forest Fields recreation field, I cry as I turn in to our cul-de-sac. I continue the crying in the shower and as I attempt to dry my hair, I cry more lying down in bed to get some doctor-ordered sleep, I cry as I give up on rest and drive back to the hospital to be with my child.

I feel that I've had my baby taken from me. At three months old she's not the bouncing chubby bundle I was promised; she's a poorly, bony little mite and my fighting for her health since her arrival in my arms has left me completely broken. I spent the nine months of my pregnancy falling in love with her and the power she now holds over my heart is terrifying to me. With a jolt I realise I've spent the time since I realised something was wrong with her – or maybe the whole time since her birth – completely blocking my heart off and distancing myself, just in case I wake up one day and she's not there. It occurs to me that now I barely utter her name out loud: I refer to her as 'The Baby' rather than 'Elfie', as if taking myself away from her this way makes it less likely that she will break my heart.

Finally, with a diagnosis of the incredibly rare genetic

condition congenital adrenal hyperplasia secondary to 3-beta-hydroxysteroid dehydrogenase deficiency (try saying that after a couple of wines) – we had more chance of winning the lottery than having a baby with this disease, would you believe – we are allowed home. After Elfie's ten-day stay in hospital, tests confirm that thankfully she is indeed a she (no awkward Facebook updates required), and though our life for the foreseeable will involve administering six different types of medication on the daily and learning how to inject our twelve-week old baby, things are looking up. Elfie will be healthy, we will be OK.

With the exception of the medical staff we've dealt with in hospital, I am so angry and disappointed at the care and help I was given as a new mother desperately worried about the health of her tiny baby. The health visitor who constantly told me not to worry, despite Elfie only putting on 2oz in a week. The paediatric nurse who told me to stop weighing Elfie every week as it would stress me out (my child was off-the-chart tiny; of course I was worried). The GP who advised me to feed her the formula sold for hungry babies, resulting in her being dehydrated when admitted to hospital. I'm so angry at these individuals who patronised me, made me feel like an overanxious mother mithering over a perfectly healthy baby, when she should have received urgent medical attention when I first raised my concerns.

I've always held people in positions of authority – doctors, police officers, teachers – in high esteem, and have trusted their advice and followed it to the letter. But this experience changes me, turns me into a person who knows it's OK to question things I'm told that go against my instincts or better judgement. This begins when we arrive home after our stay in hospital to a note from one of the health visitors who, three weeks ago, had told me with a blasé attitude to stop obsessing over my baby's weight. She writes that she's sorry we missed our appointment and has heard we're in hospital and hopes Elfie is well. Her mobile phone number is at the bottom: I ring her and tell her that if I ever hear from her again I will lose my mind. I hang up the phone and burst into tears; nobody can ever make the last few weeks of our life better, but being able to vent my sadness has helped.

A week later a tummy bug lands us back in hospital. Elfie's diagnosis means that not only will she be on a regimen of cortisol treatment for the rest of her life, but also that should she fall ill with an everyday sickness it could prove fatal for her. We're admitted back onto the children's ward but are swiftly moved when the staff realise how poorly she is. It's decided that the safest place for her at this time, for its sterility and lack of infection risk, is the paediatric oncology ward, a place I immediately dread going into as I can anticipate the amount of sadness we'll find there. Contrary to my assumption, though, our time there turns out to be possibly the best thing that could have happened to us.

Since Elfie's diagnosis and stays in various children's hospitals or paediatric wards, from Nottingham's Queen's Medical Centre to Great Ormond Street, I've learned that children are fighters like no others on this planet. Their optimism and pure zest for life is infectious; their hope and love unparalleled. They have lived the shortest time on the planet yet impart the biggest lessons – to laugh, love and hope. I see this in action for the first time on the oncology ward at the QMC and immediately make a promise never to feel sorry for myself ever again. I meet a child who, at the age of six, is on his second round of chemotherapy to treat leukaemia. Over tea in the parents' kitchen I chat to his dad, who tells me with a resigned nod that this is the last chance they've got, the last fight they're going to have. They're hopeful, he says with a smile, but who knows?

I return to Elfie's bedside knowing that, though we've got it bad, we can get through whatever her condition will throw at us. We're the lucky ones. We don't have acute myeloid leukaemia, we don't have a tumour or rounds of chemotherapy to tackle. We have a dodgy adrenal gland and a lifelong prescription for cortisol: easy-peasy. We can handle it, no bother. Elfie will grow up to be a healthy little girl and that's the main thing; she will grow up. She'll be on medication but she'll have the chance to see her first birthday. And at that point, drinking weak tea in the kitchen on the oncology ward, that feels like something to celebrate.

In the following weeks I become somewhat obsessed with Elfie's medical condition. Her consultant, an adrenal specialist based at the QMC who loves Harry Potter, tells me she'd estimate there are 180 people in the world with Elfie's disease. That becomes a subject of wonderment for me, that we've been anointed as the family to deal with this situation, we're the chosen ones. On our return home from hospital I mindlessly watch *The Jeremy Kyle Show* through tired eyes and wonder if any of the families on the show could cope with the hand we've been dealt: the various medications, the blood glucose monitors, the many consultants with their medical jargon. Will and I laugh as each new consult-ant we're introduced to enquires as to our jobs before they launch into their explanations of what our daughter's situation is; one of the more friendly doctors tells us this is so they can gauge our level of medical knowledge and understanding. Chuckling to my husband in a rare moment of togetherness, I explain to him that we're huge fans of cheesy TV hospital dramas, so probably have a better medical lexicon than most.

Looking back with the benefit of hindsight, I can see that this is definitely the beginning of the end of our marriage. I'm not sure of how a couple should perfectly deal with the near-death of and subsequent diagnosis of a life-threatening genetic condition in their newborn baby, but I'm pretty sure that not to discuss the deep and long-lasting ramifications of this with your husband is not the way to do it. The wall I started building as soon as I realised Elfie was ill gets higher, the reinforcements tighter. Living now back in Nottingham, I have precious few friends with whom to discuss the emotional impact of Elfie's illness, and any attempt from my parents to prise my box of emotions open is met with a shutdown. The situation is too painful to address, so it gets relegated to a place where I can forget about it, and together with Will I return to a life of domestic unhappiness (he immediately returns to his usual eighty-hour working weeks) and snatched superficial chats over sofa dinners.

Elfie is healthy, that's all that matters, and we try to find our new normal.

CHAPTER SIX

A Royal Change of Lifestyle

Being a mum is really hard. Much harder than I thought it would be. I can't be arsed to make any cakes, for a start, so all thoughts of being a 'baking mum' go out the window – the little broken sleep I'm getting firmly putting paid to that – and living in a place where the few people I know are at work during my monotonous days of baby talk means I don't get to socialise as much as I thought I would. I find the endless cycle of feed, wind, change, nap, cry incredibly boring, and start to resent the fact that this tiny little person drains so much from me without giving anything close to a thank-you. As someone who needs quarterly perform-ance reviews and praise from her bosses to stay motivated, I am left feeling down in the dumps by what feels like a never-ending slog of giving everything I have. My new boss is a teeny-tiny love dictator; not only does she steal my sleep and my sanity but I also feel bruised by how close I came to losing her. I wonder if I'm ever going to be able to get over the fear of losing her again.

I try going to local baby groups but struggle to find ones that suit me: I'm too young to slot into the suburban mummy sensory play/organic/Annabel Karmel meet-ups (though I do try to pretend I'm interested in Vanessa's latest 4 x 4 saga like the best of them) and am too old for the council-run 'young mum' sessions. I find sitting around in church halls incredibly tedious and can't understand why I'm expected to suddenly make connections with other mums, purely because we have the fact we've given birth in common. Having to spend a boring two hours on a Tuesday morning dissecting another baby's toilet habits when I don't even want to discuss those of my own child, all the while nibbling on a plate of stale biscuits? It's not for me, so I sack off all forced get-togethers and decide that home is a much safer place to be.

We move house, a decision that's once again taken in pursuit of my husband's burgeoning career, on the day that Prince William and Kate Middleton marry. Though now a married and sensible twenty-five-year-old in possession of rational thought, I'm borderline gutted about this: having spent the ages of seven to fourteen firmly believing I had a good chance of marrying Prince William (I spent far too many school hours daydreaming about what I'd say the first time I would meet my new grand-mother-in-law, the Queen), I can't quite believe he's off the market. And that we have to waste our wedding bank holiday heaving boxes around the country instead of cooing over the Alexander McQueen dress and mid-length veil.

But it has to be done. After nine months living in Nottingham we have conceded that the best jobs for Will are located in London, and though he's given it his best shot it's just too diffi-cult for him to travel to and from the capital by train three times a week.

A Royal Change of Lifestyle

I wish I could pretend I am excited about moving house so soon after we last hefted all our belongings up the M1, especially with a brand-new baby in tow, but that would be a lie: I am dreading it. And as time is of the essence, we haven't yet had time to source a new house or even work out where in the vicinity we can afford to live, so it's with trepidation that we rent out our Midlands home once more and move into my parents' tiny granny annexe at the bottom of their garden near Milton Keynes.

I'm sure there are many things on the list of what brand-new parents want in their home when starting a new family, and we were lucky to have the basics. We had a roof over our heads, means of income (just about – statutory maternity pay does not go far), food on our plates and a loving family surrounding us. But what we also have is a home that is currently two rooms and a cupboard bathroom. All three of us share a tiny bedroom and our living area is a small room with a tiny kitchen, a countertop microwave oven and camping hob, two-seater sofa and foldaway table. Calling our new living situation 'cosy' would be generous but any other alternative description feels too negative, and the white wood cladding on the walls when paired with the log burner could at least be termed 'rustic', I suppose.

Claustrophobic is what it actually is, but as a saving grace Will is offered a full-time and permanent job in west London. And I, driven further mad by living in a two-room home with a rapidly growing baby, decide it's time for me to rejoin the workforce as well. After doing a bit of scouting around online, I find myself a great four-day-a-week freelance gig working in London as a digital manager for the magazine of a well-known Scandinavian homewear brand, a job that seems perfect for me as I endeavour to decorate a wardrobe-sized home on a shoe-string-sized budget.

I worry what life will be like, back in the workforce. Clocking in, clocking out . . . the Dolly Parton 9–5 in motion. Will I remember how to be part of a team, how to adhere to office etiquette? How will it feel to make not one cup of tea but six each time I go to a kitchen? I look at Elfie, my now chubby nine-month-old, and I wonder if it's the right thing to do. I feel I'm failing her by giving up on pursuing full-time motherhood (wasn't it always my dream to be the SAHM, the ultimate acronym?), but as her mum I don't think I'm the best person to be at home with her, either. The days feel endlessly monotonous and I resort to Baby Einstein DVDs way more than I should, the mesmerising swirl of shapes and colours on a background providing more stimulation for Elfie than her mother listlessly drinking a cup of tea on the sofa. Will works most weekends, so I don't even have a Saturday and Sunday to look forward to, and with few friends in the local area there's nobody to call for a glass of wine or sympathetic shoulder to sob on. With no cash in the bank and a bored mind, work seems like a sensible option.

Elfie's health still worries me no end and I feel incredibly responsible for her wellness. At the same time as I desperately need to escape my life I also feel the strongest urge to remain by her side, feeling like I'm the only one who shoulders the responsibility of her. It's happened this way completely by accident: as the 'non-working' parent the onus is on me to ferry her around from hospital appointment to pharmacy, to drop everything should she show even a hint of illness. As her mother of course I'm happy to take on this role, but by God is it exhausting.

The first night I plan to be away from Elfie after her diagnosis is for the occasion of my sister-in-law's hen do in London. Elfie is cranky, clingy and sad, which I put down to an inconsequential sniffle, cheerily waving goodbye as I leave her with my mum and a couple of cooing dinner guests. I hop in a taxi wearing a face full of make-up and, in an incredibly rare occurrence, shoes that aren't my battered old Converse All Stars, feeling exhilarated to be in the company of people I'm not related or married to. I'm off to celebrate Emma's final night as a single gal, an evening that's sure to be tons of fun: a Soho bar followed by drinks and dancing and, most importantly, a blissful night alone in a hotel room snagged cheaply through my husband's work. I've almost started to relax and have nearly finished my train gin-in-a-tin as we approach Euston, the excitement of the big city and my night ahead giving me butterflies.

My phone buzzes in my handbag, one that's, pleasingly, much smaller than the hefty nappy bag I've become used to: I answer the call; it's my mum and she sounds worried.

'Elfie's not right,' Mum says. 'I don't want you to panic but she's been sick. I think she needs you.'

Of course she needs me, I'm her mother, I think. My heart breaks a little as I think of my tiny girl at nine months old, confused, feeling poorly without her mum to comfort her. I can hear her grizzling in the background, and though my shoulders slump at the thought of the missed night of fun I've so been anticipating I drink the last of the gin and reassure my mum I'll be home soon.

I stride up the ramp at Euston and on to the station concourse. I'm worried and my hands are shaking. Having not been able to make head nor tail of the online train timetable, I scan the departures boards with blurred eyes. Finally locating the first train home – it leaves in a thankful five minutes – I turn on my heel and, in a move that would be humorous if I weren't making it for the reason of my daughter's health, head back to the platform I've just left. I text a few people: my mum, telling her I'll be home soon. My sister-in-law, telling her to have a sickly sambuca for me. My husband, letting him know that his daughter will soon be en route to hospital.

In the years since I've become a single parent, returning home to my children from wherever I am in the country has proved itself to be a process that is far and beyond more difficult than anything I've ever known. I like my own company, I always have, and I believe that spending time alone (particularly when life solo with two kids is so intense) is good for my mental well-being. By and large I enjoy the time I get to relax, socialise and remember the person I was before I became 'Mum'. But no matter who I'm with, what I'm doing and where I'm going, that period of time when I'm travelling back towards my children or waiting for them to return to me is literally the most excruciating time.

I've never known anything like it. I know I'll be reunited with my children within hours, if not minutes, but for the short time I'm waiting to get to them I feel a physical ache. My arms feel empty and a hundred times lighter than usual, anticipating the feeling of enveloping them while I squeeze them so tightly I may never let go. I have been known to get anxious and desperate in these times: if my husband is ever late returning them or I run into an unexpected travel delay there is sobbing, desperate racking heaves as I cry, 'I need my babies.'

It was this empty-armed feeling I was trying to make sense of as I hopped up and down in my seat on the 18.43 back from Euston, willing the train to go faster, to hurry up as I sped back home towards my poorly baby. My fellow passengers must have thought me mad (or prematurely pissed) as I looked at them with a clenched jaw and wild eyes, trying desperately to distract myself from the thoughts racing through my head. Elfie was much stronger than she had been a few months ago, but with all her life-preserving medication being taken orally, if she'd been sick she'd need someone – me – to give her a top-up – and quickly. All I wanted to do was sweep her up in my arms and hug her until she was better.

I jumped into what was going to feel like the slowest cab ever, lugging my weekend bag containing the evening's unworn Topshop (sale) dress behind me. Fifteen minutes later we were home and I quickly thrust a tenner into my cabbie's hand and then burst through the front door to my baby. She was better than I'd expected, awake and alert, smiling weakly at her mama. Behind my own mother were three of her friends, clutching glasses of Sauvignon Blanc, all set to enjoy their Saturday night dinner party. They knew nothing of my panic as I smiled through gritted teeth, wondering how I could extract my car from the melee on the driveway with the least disruption to the party. Dad saved the day, telling me I could take his wheels: a sporty speedy white machine that I'd been desperate to take out ever since he'd bought it – he'd always said no, of course, at least until now.

I tried to be pleased that I'd at least be driving Elfie to hospital in style as I strapped her in, eyeing the cream leather interior with anxious eyes. There's literally no better way of ensuring a child will vomit than putting them in a situation where it would be highly inconvenient for them to do so, and true to form she threw up five minutes into our journey. That's my girl.

Her eyes closed and I started to panic, knowing I needed to get her medication into her as quickly as possible.

The A & E department at Milton Keynes hospital is a little walk away from the car park, a fact that panicked me on this day and has annoyed me on many visits since. Feeling like an entitled dick (but not knowing what else to do – I didn't think I had time to fanny around with collecting car park tickets and hefting my very poorly daughter across wintery tarmac), I slammed my dad's sports car into one of the ambulance bays. Praying nobody would stop me to ask awkward questions as I struggled to unstrap Elfie from a vomit-soaked car seat, I hefted her on to my hip, stopping only to grab her nappy bag and lock the car door.

Elfie is what's called a 'Red Box Patient', meaning that she has an alert on her name so that, should we have the need to whisk her to hospital in an emergency situation, she skips triage and sees a doctor immediately. I said a quick prayer of thanks to the Nottingham consultant who had helped me set this process up as I laid her out on an examination table in front of the A & E doctor five minutes after our arrival.

I've found in my seven years as the parent of a child with an incredibly rare disease that it's never easy to deal with medical professionals unless they know her case intimately. Doctors generally know best – of course they do, they're doctors – but in Elfie's case there's a protocol that must be followed to make her better in situations like this one, where she's fallen quickly and gravely ill. The only problem is that these protocols generally differ from a hospital's standard operating procedure, meaning medical professionals don't like to follow them lest they land themselves and their trust in medical and legal bother. So alongside learning all about my daughter's new condition I've also had to learn the best way to advocate for her health, which often involves quite awkward conversations with professionals who think they know better than me – and who, having not dropped out of university *ahem*, by and large do. But not when it comes to Elfie.

If Elfie's vomited or is otherwise ill it's usually because her medication is no longer in her body or she needs an extra dose of it, and as a consequence her blood sugar is too low; therefore to kick-start the healing process she needs an injection quick-smart in her thigh and some glucose in her mouth. On this Saturday night when I should have been sipping on margaritas in a Soho gay bar, I knew this: I had a letter from our Nottingham consultant saying words to that effect, too. But that wasn't how the A & E doctor we were with wanted to run her treatment that evening. She told me, very kindly it has to be said, that when babies present with Elfie's symptoms they must be treated per the hospital's protocol. Their plan was to put a line into Elfie's hand by which they'd slowly deliver her medication, taking tests all night until she was well again.

I knew this was wrong, that putting a line in Elfie's hand would cause her an unnecessary amount of pain and would mean her recovery would be too slow. I couldn't just sit back and watch them come at my daughter with unnecessary big needles.

I put my foot down, an action that was fairly authoritative as I was still wearing my going-out shoes. 'That's not what needs to happen here,' I told her. 'You can clearly see in Elfie's notes from Nottingham that she simply needs a hydrocortisone injection in her thigh. I don't consent to a line.'

The doctor shook her head.

'I can't do that,' she said. 'As her mother, if this is the direction you want to take then I won't stand in your way, but I can't administer the drugs myself. You'll have to do it.'

I looked at her incredulously.

'You want me to give her the injection?' I asked. 'Me, the knackered mum who's been to London and back this evening in the space of an hour and is wearing shoes that are clearly too uncomfortable?'

She nodded her assent.

'Fine,' I said. 'Have you got any of those blue gloves?'

I'd only ever injected an orange before but that didn't seem to matter, so fuelled by the adrenaline that had come from the rush to be with my sick baby was I, not to mention the sickening drive to the hospital and the panicked discussions with the doctors. At that point, if I'd been asked to scale the hospital walls and moon the people in the multi-storey car park I probably would have found it in me to do it, Spider-Man style. My little girl needed me to be brave and I was going to do her proud.

It's not easy, fiddling about with Elfie's emergency medication. It comes in a glass vial with a lid that needs to be snapped off with a bit of fabric, otherwise you find yourself picking tiny shards of glass out of the pad of your thumb for days to come. You then pop a wide needle on the end of a syringe to allow you to draw up the solution, before switching the needle to a finer one more suited to a baby's thighs and flicking it to get rid of any air that may have accumulated (and feeling like you're on *Holby City* while you're at it). You then hold your child's thigh as still as possible – hopefully with someone else dealing with the flailing upper body portion – and direct the needle in, pushing down on the syringe to administer the correct amount of medication.

I'm not sure 'fucking terrifying' is the correct medical term for this process but it's how I felt at this moment.

The doctor, seeing me perform the dance of the syringe, belatedly realised that I meant complete business and that, come hell or high water, I intended to inject my daughter. 'It's OK!' she said, 'please, let me.'

I side-eyed her in a way I'd never side-eyed anyone before (and probably haven't since). 'No thank you,' I said. 'This is against your protocol and I don't want you getting into trouble. We don't need your help.'

I plunged the needle into Elfie's thigh as she shrieked, injecting her medication and then popping the used syringe in a cardboard kidney-shaped tray that a nurse had thoughtfully provided. Using a cotton ball to stem the pinhead of red that had appeared at the injection site, I swept her up in my arms, offering her dummy as she snuggled into me. She was quiet. She was going to be OK.

We were released from hospital after clear test results four hours later, in a move I had predicted to the doctor on our arrival. From watching and studying the doctors who buzzed and fussed over Elfie during our original hospital admissions, I'd known that having her emergency medication injected would bring her back up to health – and I wasn't wrong. The A & E doctor conceded the same as she released us and watched us skulk back to our illegally parked car in the cold night air. I felt empowered that evening, in a completely different way to how I'd expected. I'd anticipated an inspired wild night on the tiles with my sister-in-law and her friends, a lot of drink and dancing, perhaps a bit of karaoke; I had imagined myself coming back from the evening remembering my old child-free self and perhaps being able to take forward her confidence and joie de vivre (two personality traits I seemed recently to have lost in my new position as borderline reclusive stay-at-home mum).

But instead I felt energised by the fact that, though I'd initially failed my daughter by not advocating strongly enough to medical professionals when she was a newborn, this time I'd thoroughly asserted my position as a strong and capable mother. I was a lion, a fierce protector, a force of nature. I was going to protect my child and I did, I really did. I had never felt prouder as I looked that night at Elfie, my slightly hot and sticky but most definitely healthy baby girl. I might have stabbed her in the thigh with a really sharp stick but I was walking on air and I didn't even have an armful of overpriced hen-do drinks to thank for it.

With this frantic experience of A & E and my craving to remember life outside a medicalised version of motherhood, it's no wonder I was so desperate to get back out to work. My new job started three weeks after the first time I injected my daughter and I wasn't really sure what to expect. I hoped I'd be able to handle the site redesign I was managing; the project cost more than my first house but that excited me more than anything else, and I was looking forward to getting back into what I felt was the real world full of real 3D people. I was excited to have more than my child's excreta to talk about at the next mummy meet-up I went to.

I didn't bank on loving the job, though, as much as I did. To understand this I feel you have to understand some more about my career thus far. Though I had loved my work before, I was always very much more into the social aspect of it, the after-work drinks and friends I made in the office. My tenacity and experience made sure that I did fairly well for myself, but throughout my career I always felt as if I was somewhat waiting in the wings. I knew something bigger, motherhood, was coming my way, so I always felt like I didn't need to throw myself into my job 100 per cent.

Until I became a mother and realised that, actually, I did.

God, I'd missed the validation of a job. I'd missed the joviality of an office. Missed the socialisation of a team. I pined for the importance that I once had as a manager, the way my ideas were seen as valid and implementable. I needed that meeting once every three months with my manager, a totally emotionless guy called Matt who, though he made me feel pretty shitty at the time, gave me worlds more validation than the baby who screamed at me and stole all my sleep.

Sitting at my new desk that first week in my new Shoreditch office, I had a text from my mum. She was at home with the baby but was the one to ask,

Are you OK?

I'd woken up at five that morning to get the 6.45 a.m. train into town, but I felt like I was flying.

Am I OK?

I asked.

You've got to be kidding me, compared with my life at home with the baby I feel like I'm on a spa break.

And so it went. I missed Elfie but felt I was serving my family much better by being in an office earning an impossibly large-sounding £250 a day freelance wage, taking Fridays off nominally to spend with my daughter but in reality making the most of my time assuaging my working-mum guilt in (non-sale) GAP and Topshop. I did well in my job, won the agency new business and made a success of the projects I'd already been given, but I couldn't help but wonder if I was really doing the right thing. Plus, as I was still the parent-in-charge, the one to dive home from work for illnesses and hospital appointments, I was in a perpetual state of knackeredness and spent as much time trying to stay awake as I did working.

What's the one thing a barely-coping working mum needs? A babysitter? A bit more money to treat herself? An actual spa day rather than a relaxing eight hours at a desk?

NAH – you want to give her a new baby to look after.

And that's exactly what happened, a clean twenty-two months after Elfie appeared.

Since having Elfie and starting my new media job we'd moved to the town next to my parents' village. In a sleep-deprived state we'd gone for a fancy town-centre apartment over a sensible suburban semi, and though there was no garden we were within striding distance of both Boots and three pubs we'd never have time to frequent.

Town centre living suited us to a point. It was handy being so close to the Co-op supermarket and a couple of lovely parks, but our upstairs neighbour was a lorry driver who got picked up for his shift by an early-rising pal at five every morning. Nice for him, I'm sure, but our nine-month-old daughter woke for the day each and every time Mr Upstairs left for work. We didn't know how to make it any better: though many a polite pow-wow was had with him to explain the incredibly noisy leaving-the-house situation, even his softest socks on the wooden floor and his carefullest shutting of the front door would wake our slumbering babe, ensuring we were all awake at an hour that made us want to stick our heads in the (new) oven. It wasn't his fault, he was a lovely man, but God I hated him, his bloody early starts and that apartment.

After a solid four months of sleep deprivation and a promise from my ex-husband that two children under two would equal a life with more equilibrium, I got pregnant. It didn't take much – I like to say that I'd have to be protected from a sneeze if I didn't want to add to my brood – but we were mostly happy with the news. As one of four siblings, Will was excited to add another child to the mix, and to be honest I was so tired out by Elfie's early rising that I would have agreed to giving birth to Hitler if it had meant a good night's sleep may have been on the horizon. Spoiler: it wasn't.

Mixing my pregnancy with work and the 6.45 a.m. commute proved incredibly difficult, and before too long I finished my

Shoreditch freelance project and went out on my own. I was incredibly, bone-crunchingly exhausted throughout both of my pregnancies – I recall eating many a meal lying down in bed because lifting a fork from the table to my face was just too much effort – so being able to nap at will without the distraction of an office was a real bonus. I say nap at will, but there was still a toddler Elfie to consider at this point: she was perhaps the least sympathetic person in my life when it came to the extreme pregnancy exhaustion I suffered, even worse than her father, who liked to chuckle while he reminded me 'You're not disabled, you're pregnant.' I remember one memorable occasion at about eighteen weeks when, while cleaning the house, I suddenly just couldn't move further than the couch and had to lie down among the cushions lest I pass out from exhaustion. Trying to entertain Elfie, who was just a bit too young to give a shit about Mr Tumble, I turned the TV on and valiantly tried to direct her attention in that vague direction.

'Look, honey!' I exclaimed, as tired tears coursed their way down my cheeks. 'What's in his spotty sack?!'

She responded by poking me in the eye. 'MUMMY CRY!' she delightedly shouted. 'HAHAHAHAH!!'

My pregnancy with Hux, though knackering, was uneventful. I was thrilled that he'd spent the entire time head down, ready, I was sure, to engage with my cervix and make up for my former Caesarean and the ensuing medical nightmare by happily flying out of my vagina into the world to meet us all.

BUT LIFE DOESN'T WORK THAT WAY, ALICE.

I start having contractions during my thirty-ninth week, on my husband's thirtieth birthday. We're at a pub for lunch with friends and family and, boozeless and with a child lodged some-where near my cervix, I am very unamused to be the fat and fed-up designated driver.

I had made a few comments about my discomfort over the course of the day but, feeling very aware that I was not to ruin The Big 30, I mostly kept my grumbles to myself. My second pregnancy had been so different from the first – what with being a mother of one already, there was a distinct lack of time and space this time to whine too much about my bone-crunching exhaustion, and I wanted my birth to follow the same vibe of being low-key, relaxed and without fuss.

But these things never go to plan, do they?

They say that when you first meet your baby you're hit with a massive wall of love, an unmistakable hit of 'Wow, that's my child, that's the one I'm going to treasure for ever.' I've heard that theory from many sources, from Hollywood and magazines and from friends, too, sensible friends who tell the truth about these things. Which was why it bothered me for a long time that I didn't experience this lightning bolt of love and recognition when I gave birth to Elfie; her arrival was an altogether more confusing mix of 'WTF,' 'Have I really done the right thing here?' and 'What is this weird waxy white shit all over my child?'

I always expected those feelings to come later, in the times we'd quietly spend at home getting to know each other over hours of breastfeeding and Netflix box sets. I hoped that one day, maybe six weeks down the line while cradling her to my breast in my finest Primark post-birth PJs, I'd have that moment when I went YES. She's my child. I'm here to love her. You know how it went with Charlotte in *Sex and the City*? When she looks at the photo of baby Lily from China and says 'THAT'S OUR BABY' while grabbing Harry's tie, causing a million women worldwide to sob? That's the feeling I was waiting for.

But with all the nonsense over her not weighing enough, her ensuing health problems and my anxiety over life in general after she left the hospital, we never got there. The moment I craved remained just that: a moment I continued to crave.

It wasn't that I didn't love her. I did. I really did. It just didn't happen like they all told me. Without the actual experience of having a lightning bolt strike my heart, I felt like I was just going through the motions of love. I was still there, her mother, cradling her in a hospital bed as she screamed her little heart out at 4 a.m., whispering into her downy head that I'd give anything to take her pain away, but our love felt flawed and sullied with the mass that had come before it. It wasn't the pure, all-encompassing, heart-expanding love I'd been told to expect, and I missed it.

One of the biggest disappointments I have about my early stages of being a mum is that nobody told me that it was OK to feel this way. In one way or another a woman's entrance into motherhood isn't going to be seamless, whether that's health issues with mum or baby, post-natal depression or just a massive dose of sleep deprivation. It's true what they say, that being a mum is the absolute hardest job of them all, and chances are you *won't* be the magazine mum with good hair, a lack of eye bags and a non-soiled outfit, staring beatifically down at the cherubic child in your arms. The real picture of motherhood is more grey skin, vomited-on jumpers and a snot-covered baby. And that's fine! That's how it's supposed to be.

But hindsight is a wonderful thing and back then I felt such a lot of guilt that I didn't completely and utterly believe the sun shone out of my baby's beautiful bottom. I loved her, I believed she was incredibly special and the most gorgeous little person I'd ever seen, but still. Where was that moment when my baby was first placed in my arms and I suddenly realised I loved her? Fair enough, at the time of her birth I was flat on my back, numb from the boobs down, and she was wafted under my nose rather than tenderly placed in my arms, so it was never going to happen as in the movies. But I still felt entirely short-changed.

My unconditional bolt of all-encompassing love for Elfie came when she was about a year and a half old. We were doing something totally unremarkable, babbling to each other while I cleaned and she played, and it hit me all of a sudden. This was my baby, I'd given birth to her, she was mine and I was her mummy. It felt almost as if I'd been playing at being a mum for a long while and now, all of a sudden, I'd just become one. It felt like everyone had said: it was the best most heart-warming sensation of warmth and completeness, of happiness and joy, feeling like it was emanating from every pore of my pregnant and tired face. I hugged her to me and cried; she gummed the tears from my face and stuck her finger up my nose. I laughed: this was love.

When Hux was born, not wanting to wait eighteen months to go ga-ga for him I was determined to do everything I could to fall in love from the get-go. As I'd had a Caesarean section with Elfie I really wanted to have a vaginal birth this time round, so I read reams of information on VBACS (Vaginal Birth After Caesarean), learning everything I could about the risks and pitfalls. I'd been in and out of hospital near the end of the pregnancy, for palpitations – did you know that when you have your heart monitored via ECG a young handsome doctor puts sticky pads all over your boobs? Now I did! – and the Braxton Hicks I found myself saddled with were out of this world.

I went into labour proper right after Will's birthday, spending nights in the bath trying to quell the pains in my tightening abdomen. Worried about the chance of uterine abruption (when your old Caesarean-section scar splits during labour – perhaps learning everything I could about VBACS was not the best idea – ouch) I hurried myself into hospital as soon as I could, which turned out to be 2cm dilated. Having never even got to this stage of labour with Elfie, I was pretty proud of myself and gleefully accepted the offer of a stretch and sweep from the midwife who admitted me on to the antenatal ward. That feeling continued until she somehow managed to fit her entire hand inside my vagina to reach my (apparently set-back) cervix, making me feel like a cow in a James Herriot novel: yet another thing they neglect to tell us about real-life childbirth.

I was placed opposite another labouring mother on the ward and we waited for things to progress. I was in pain, yes, but it was manageable and I was trying to hold off on pain relief until shit got serious further down the line, as I knew it very much would. I dealt with my contractions by breathing deeply, closing my eyes and imagining waves crashing on a beach. Interspersed with endless episodes of *The Office* on my iPad.

The other mum-to-be really quite terrified me. On all fours, she was bellowing like a moose, screaming at her partner and sucking on the can of gas and air as if her life depended on it.

After a very loud examination (midwife: 'I haven't touched you yet, please stop screaming') she was carted off to the labour ward, my ideas of calmly and quietly breathing through labour all but leaving the room with her.

'Is she OK?' I asked the midwife on her return.

'Oh, she'll be fine,' she promised me. 'Some women find 3cm difficult.'

Twenty-four hours later and I was also finding 3cm difficult, just without the mooing and midwife-directed obscenities. I was still doing my breathing and *Office*-watching but I was tired, my contractions were proving pretty ineffectual and my baby's heartbeat was starting to slow with my tightening abdomen. Giving me another stretch and sweep, my consultant produced a really long pointy stick and said she could either pierce my waters there and then to bring on more contractions or she could book me on to the Caesarean list for that day. Baulking at the thought of anything sharper than a hand burrowing its way inside me, I said I'd take the lovely surgeon cutting my tummy open over the scary-sounding breaking of waters, thank you, and happily watched as a cannula was inserted in my (non-tweeting, I insisted) hand.

Having been awake for three days by this point, I don't remember this Caesarean as well as my first one. I recall the anaesthetist, who congratulated me on my excellent banter – I liked him – and the fact that my husband took ages to arrive because he was initially taken into the wrong theatre and seated at the head of a lady who wasn't me. I remember being given medicine to help my uterus contract on account of it being 'flabby', my surgeon having no qualms over my having internal body image issues and being warned that I would probably be violently sick. (Me, prone and completely numbed on the operating table: 'No! I don't want to be sick! I've just washed my hair!')

Huxley William arrived on 16 May at 3.04 p.m., weighing 7lbs 5oz. He was immediately alert and beautiful but was whisked off straight away to begin tests to check that he didn't have the same genetic condition as Elfie.

Being stitched up without my baby there was the slowest process I've ever endured and I silently cried as my now child-less belly was fixed and cleaned. Arriving on the ward, I saw him being cuddled and cradled by his dad and immediately lowered my gown for skin-to-skin contact.

We spent a week in hospital while Hux was tested and, when it came to our bonding, there couldn't have been a better place for us to do it in peace with no distractions. We were on a ward with five other mothers and their babies, an experience unlike anything I'd known before. The woman opposite me had birthed a very dinky baby with jaundice and was waiting for her colour to come up: she was one of the most interesting people I've ever come across. A heavily tattooed woman, she had very outspoken opin-ions about the books she was reading (she got through two of the *Fifty Shades* tomes in our week together) and told me all about her very interesting career as a butcher in the massively dodgy part of town. She didn't have a shower for the entire week we were in hospital and I didn't see her visiting husband utter one word in that time. If Hux and I could bond in this place, the hottest May on record in an environment where our biggest topics of conversa-tion were Christian Grey and the best cuts of beef you could get outside of Smithfield market, we were going to be OK.

My dad spent the week cooking up gorgeous things for me to eat – lamb tagines accompanied by mini bottles of champagne and the loveliest pasta dishes, accompanied by tiny tins of gin – so I wasn't left chewing on the hospital's watery carrots and dodgy sausages (though I was so hungry I ate them too). Hux and I did nothing but sleep, eat and cuddle, a sharp contrast to Elfie's first weeks of life, which were altogether more filled with worry, sleep deprivation and vomit. Looking back at the warm, sticky ward with one toilet to share between six women who had just given birth, I feel sad that this was the slightly whiffy location of our first week together, but needs must.

Having already had a Caesarean, this time round I was so much more chilled about the post-birth process. Though once again I didn't get the magnificently Zen vaginal birth I'd planned, I still wanted to go as natural as possible. Skin to skin, co-sleeping, breastfeeding. Which I guess was the reason I turned down the liquid morphine when the friendly midwife popped into my cubicle at twelve hours post-section, hefty painkillers not partnering with the attachment parenting vibe I was going for. IDIOT. I spent days in pain, a lot of pain: if you have a Caesarean please take all the painkillers; you're going to need them.

God, though natural birth is hard, Caesareans are hard, too. If anyone ever suggests your C-section birth was less difficult than pushing a baby out through one's vag I suggest you punch them in the face: getting your abdomen sliced hip to hip and a child extracted from the resulting wound is no bloody walk in the park. It hurts. It really, really hurts. And anyway, whichever way you grow and expel a child out of your body you're a freaking warrior.

All pregnancies are hard and I have absolutely no qualms about saluting every single woman who's been through the process of bearing new life. My old CEO said it best, when I asked him at twenty weeks pregnant after spending most of the day running around London for meetings, whether it would be OK for me to go home and work out the rest of the day in bed. 'You're creating a person from scratch,' he told me. 'This little thing inside you is leeching away all the goodness you have. Of course you can go home and lie down whenever you need to.'

I always say that, for the most part, if carrying and giving birth to children were up to men then as a species we'd quickly become extinct. There's literally nothing sexy about childbirth or the process you go through to get there, with each and every stage being more humiliating and dehumanising than the last. The first post-Caesarean highlight I personally encountered was on the hospital ward with Hux, that hot and stuffy room where six of us tried to simply get through the days with our child-ravaged battered bodies until we'd finally be allowed home. We had the holy grail on our ward – a loo with not only a shower but a window as well – and though I felt like I was dousing myself in MRSA each time I washed, I was at least happy to be able to view a slice of the outside world. My embarrassment came three days post-section, as I tried for my first successful bowel movement.

I'm not sure if you've ever tried to poo post-abdominal surgery but it's really quite a tricky thing. You find you feel all weird where once you didn't, shuffling around trying not to jimmy things that should be left alone. It's astonishing to realise which are the muscles you need to use to poo; so many of them are located where your baby has just exited, but you have to do what you have to do and though this was not the case with me (as I was anyway enjoying an extended stay at Milton Keynes General), quite often post-birth women are required to pass a stool before they're allowed to go home, like some sort of sadistic bowel movement test.

As recommended, I took a towel to the bathroom with me that day to hold against my abdomen wound, a move that, it's often suggested, will prevent any huge discomfort while straining on the loo. And three days after my operation and a good number of hearty and fibre-filled meals brought in by my dad (heartier than food from the hospital's canteen, that's for sure), I was absolutely desperate to go. So desperate was I that it wasn't even that much of a challenge, and feeling thankful I took an MRSA shower and went to put my slippers on and shuffle back to my bed. Only, taking a last glance at the bathroom, I noticed there was something wrong with the toilet. Yep, I'd managed to have such a successful bowel movement that I'd clean (or not-so-clean) blocked the loo. What an achievement, eh?

I'd like to pretend I know what I said to the nurse that day when I had to own up to clogging the U-bend but I just can't remember. All I know is that, for the next five hours, there was an 'out of order' sign on the toilet while they waited for some poor sod from maintenance to come and sort it out. And that's saying something: if you've ever had a baby you'll know the insane amount of nonsense that excretes itself from your uterus (and often down the loo) post-birth, so it is no mean feat that it was my poo that eventually broke the metaphorical camel's back and clogged the ward toilet.

Plumbing disasters aside, Hux and I had a pretty fabulous

week in hospital together. I can't tell you how wonderful it was not to worry about anything except for the bond I was supposed to create with my son, and the time we had to lie together, sleep together, get to know each other . . . It was a world away from the stress and worry I'd felt with Elfie and that was just incredible.

I had my bolt-of-lightning feeling of love with Hux on the fourth day of his life. It was the same as I'd eventually felt with Elfie, just as they all say. It happened and I immediately knew that I was his mummy and I'd do anything I could to protect this little thing; my heart would never feel the same again and I was bloody delighted at that fact. I had a son and I would walk on hot coals to make him happy.

We were told that Hux was healthy on the seventh day of being in the hospital. I wept and wept, not only for him but for the fact that I'd never have to kill myself advocating for him in the same way I had fought to advocate for Elfie. I knew that no babies came with a guarantee – you don't buy them from John Lewis, you don't get your thirty days – but this was the best news we could have hoped for in these circumstances. My little boy was 'normal' and I couldn't wait to have him at home with me, his dad and his sister.

CHAPTER SEVEN

When Children Send You Mad

In between becoming a mother to two under two and my marriage breaking down I quite literally go bonkers, struck down with an enduring and horrific case of post-natal depression accompanied by its reluctant friend, anxiety. Do I go mad because my marriage is about to end or does my marriage end because I've gone mad? I'm not sure I'll ever know.

When I came home after Hux had been born I felt like I'd spent about a year, not a week, in hospital. I'd so missed my own bed, my own sofa, making cups of tea in my own kitchen. Even though one week on from the C-section I still couldn't move well or lift anything, I just wanted to be back in my nest and readjusting to life with my family as the four of us.

The bliss of being at home was somewhat short-lived: citing the pressures of the new business, Will went back to work the day I was discharged and I moved on to the reality of getting on with life with a baby and a toddler. Which was, any way you spin it, a complete and utter shit-show: extreme sleep deprivation, mastitis, more bleeding nipples, constant nappy-changing, all the cleaning, a hideous amount of washing and, in addition, a husband to cook for and look after.

One shining light in the darkness of post-partum Mark II was the way Elfie reacted to and interacted with her new baby brother. I'd been quite worried about how she'd take my attention being directed to a mewling pile of blankets over her, and now she was a boisterous twenty-two-month-old I wasn't sure if she'd turn into some kind of Stewie-from-*Family Guy* evil genius, plotting ways to poke the new baby's eyes out and displaying them on poles in our front garden. But I realised my worries were totally misplaced as my heart expanded watching the tender way she touched him. She loved to cuddle and kiss him, soon learned how to point out his nose, ears, head and (erm, don't poke them out) eyes. Whenever he cried she ran to him, soothing him with a 'There, there bubby' and an overenthusiastic pat. Sure, there was the odd occasion when she nutted him, but I'm positive that was purely by accident.

Hux was also the most scrumptious baby on the planet, which definitely helped me slowly adjust to life with two. He was incredibly easy-going and just got on with things, feeding on demand, napping when he fancied and tolerating all the earpulls and chattering that his sister gave him. With Elfie unable to say his name, he quickly became nicknamed 'Bubby', a term that stuck around until he was old enough to tell me to stop calling him that. I'm not sure if it was all the time we had spent focusing on skin-to-skin and breastfeeding in hospital but our bond was unshakable and palpable: we co-slept snuggled in to each other, he spent his days strapped to my front in a carrier and I was absolutely head over heels in love with him. Despite the logistical difficulties and the extra responsibilities a new baby presented, he slotted into my life like that one piece of the jigsaw puzzle that had been lost under the sofa.

It takes me a while to realise the fact that I can't physically bring myself to get up in the morning isn't normal. Without even realising it I've stopped washing my hair, am only taking showers if I really have to, and don't leave the house for days if I can help it. I become obsessed with having the correct amount of food to save me visiting a shop (my stockpiles mean we'd be fine in the case of nuclear warfare), and if I have to make a pilgrimage to our local Tesco Express for milk or bread it takes me hours to work up the courage, so terrified am I of having to speak to people other than my children. I'm not sure my brain stretches to conversation outside of *In The Night Garden* and *Peppa Pig* any more. Muddy puddle chat? I'm your gal. Musing on the government's latest disaster? Nope.

My personal slovenliness extends to the house and I stop cleaning at all, a habit that is in complete contrast to my usual overzealous Monica Geller cleaning tendencies. Any tidying or cleaning feels like an effort that is just too great to make, which means the kitchen table becomes encrusted with cement-like scraps of Weetabix and days-old baked beans. The last thing I want to do is drag the hoover out of its cupboard storage space and anyway, I really don't care; I'm happy in my dirty misery.

The 2012 Olympics begin and I breathe a sigh of relief: I have a legitimate reason to spend all day, every day in front of the television with the children. Who needs to be uplifted by human company when you have Mo Farah and Bradley Wiggins to care about? An old school friend wins a gold medal as part of the men's coxless fours and I surmise that I surely can't be that much of a tragic and crazy recluse if one of my Facebook friends is an Olympic champion. Ridiculous logic: I have it in spades.

My madness becomes quite extreme and is a small taster, an entirely unamusing *amuse-bouche*, of the turbulent times to come. Living in a big and echoey house that, pre-move-in, seemed aspirational and perfect for our growing family is now suddenly fraught with danger in every room. It is a double-height barn conversion with a connected brick building containing regular-sized living space and bedrooms, and the ground-floor master bedroom suite I so lusted after looking at it in the estate agent's window now feels incredibly scary and unsafe. This room and the living room and hallway attached to it have a combined five sets of doors leading out to the courtyard garden, and I become obsessed with the idea of the house getting broken in to; a spate of burglaries are reported on our village's local Facebook page, and hunting down the white van that's been cited as being connected with the robberies becomes a full-time job. I'm like Nancy Drew, only with two kids and a massive anxiety problem.

With Will almost constantly away, I lie awake at night truly believing the thumps and trumps of the house settling are a burglar, an evil force desperate to get into my house to burgle – or, worse, rape and murder – the children and me. I don't sleep at all, and when I do it's very lightly and with a hairspray can (the internet's suggestion of a weapon for women living alone) clutched in my sweaty hands. I set up booby traps on each and every one of the doors leading out to the courtyard, certain my washing rack and mops-and-buckets leaning against them will create enough of a noise to deter any wannabe burglars or murderers trying to breach my boundaries.

A highlight of my madness comes one evening as I observe a group of youths on their BMXs from my viewpoint up in Hux's bedroom. Certain the bored fourteen-year-olds who are innocently spending the evening on their bikes are way more menacing than they appear, I become convinced they're circling the cul-de-sac with the purpose of casing my home for a future robbery.

I start shaking and crying, feeling sick, unsafe and helpless, incredibly fearful for what might come: rampaging kids banging on the front door? Sneaky burglars at the back one? I creep down the stairs on trembling legs to make sure the front door is locked – of course it is, it always is – and, slowly and making sure I can't be seen, draw all the curtains across. I leg it back upstairs and secrete myself by the same upstairs window, silently sobbing as I call my husband and ask him to come home.

He says no, he can't bring his meetings to an end because I'm needlessly paranoid about kids breaking into the house, and I resume my routine of curtain-twitching to make sure the teenagers haven't yet armed themselves with crowbars or other weapons to break into my home, my sacred sanctuary.

Not knowing what else to do, I call the police non-emergency number and once again cry down the phone, telling the kind person on the other end that I'm all alone in the house with my babies and I'm scared that the people on their bikes outside my window are going to hurt me. They soothingly tell me not to worry, it'll all be OK, and I tuck myself into the foetal position and curl up on my son's bedroom floor clutching my mobile in a bid to try to stop myself shaking.

I get up only when I see the flash of blue lights outside my window, and resume my position at the window surveillance spot to see what's happening. After chatting to the kids and waving them off on their bikes, the police officers knock on my front door.

They're met with a mess. I can't remember the last time I washed my hair, I haven't slept in weeks and the energy I've expended on my anxiety and sobbing that evening has left my face puffy and red. The policewoman takes one look at my face that's wide-eyed with distress, nods to her partner and leads me to the sofa. She sits me down and pats my hand. 'Having young children is hard,' she says. 'You don't have to worry about coping.'

I almost feel embarrassed at the tears coursing down my cheeks but I'm too scared, too sick of the tight knot of anxiety in my chest, to care about my snot-filled sobbing on her stab-vest-clad shoulder.

She continues, 'You did the right thing to call us. It's OK to feel scared, asking for help is the exact thing to do. We're here for you whenever you are worried.'

I'm pretty sure those two officers from Thames Valley Police had better things to do than attend the house of an anxiety-ridden, sleep-deprived new mother, but I could have kissed the ground they walked on. Before that point I hadn't admitted there was anything wrong with the way I felt and had just let myself go quietly crazy, stuck in my own head, which was by then in a fug of exhaustion, anxiety and despair. I thought all new mothers experienced these feelings; I thought the fact that my hair was a matted greasy bird's nest and my tired unwashed face had an unkempt grey pallor was totally normal. Were mums of newborns supposed to be able to socialise and act happy? I couldn't, didn't see how anyone was supposed to do that. I'd come to terms with the – imagined – fact that life after children was misery-filled for everyone.

The night I leaned on the police instead of my husband was when I began to detach myself from my marriage. Sure, I could have called my parents, asked my dad to come over and chase the baddies away, but I was too frightened of showing them just how scared of life I was. I didn't want them to be disappointed at the shell I'd become, worry them when they saw I wasn't adult enough to open my own curtains to look at a bunch of innocent fourteen-year-olds on their bikes. The police were my substitute husband that night and I had never felt so without a rock or an anchor. I missed my partner. I was empty and alone.

One day, not long after my police encounter, I drag my dusty laptop out and open Google with trepidation. Yes, I have one child who enjoys rising with the lark (although I've not ever met a lark who gets up at 3.45 a.m., take note Elfie) and another who is still completely dependent on my breasts, but something has to give. Something has to be done.

I type in 'post-natal depression' and go through the list of symptoms, mentally ticking them off as I go. Persistent sadness and low mood? Yep. Lack of enjoyment and loss of interest in the world? You got it. No energy and feeling tired all the time? Too right. Frightening thoughts? I have 'em in abundance.

The NHS website directs me to speak to my doctor about my feelings, which makes me feel anxious and scared all over again. It's one thing admitting how I feel to myself (and even typing it into Google), but it's quite another to speak the words out loud to another person. I'm sure I'm really not right – one whiff of my unwashed armpits would confirm that – but what if my doctor tells me to pull myself together, stop making a fuss and to get on with being a mum? Or worse, what if she tells me that yep, I really am going mad, and takes my kids away from me? I don't feel like I would win either way, but I am falling deeper into my mental-health hole, running out of options; and so, feeling horribly scared, I bite the bullet and call the GP's surgery to make an appointment.

I enter the waiting area of the surgery and fiddle with my hands until the obtrusively loud buzzer goes off and my name is announced over the intercom. I sit down opposite the GP. 'What can I do for you today?' she asks, as if she's just seated me at my table at Pizza Express and is about to serve me a Pollo Ad Astra and a glass of Pinot Grigio.

'I think I might cry now,' I say, and I do.

The thing about women with post-natal depression is that, for better or worse, a lot of us know how to fake happiness. Unless our depression is acute we still manage to get up every day and complete the tasks required of us: the bathing of our children, the cooking of their meals. The minimal house upkeep. So often we are able to pretend to our nearest and dearest that (although we find motherhood admittedly a little tricky), we are altogether pretty OK. But it is not usually the case that we're OK on the inside. On the outside there are smiles and general happiness, a hastily painted picture of a functioning mother, but on the inside we're in turmoil.

It's this picture, I assume, I presented to my GP that day, that morning when I had told myself I was going to be honest and speak the truth. It didn't work: I was wearing my mask of semi-happy functionality too well and so came away with a low-level Citalopram prescription and a request to keep my chin up. She'd decided my case wasn't worth referring for CBT (cognitive behavioural therapy) because the waiting list was too long, and that I'd probably grow out of my depression as the children got older and before I reached the top of it.

This experience was the one I was terrified of, the waggy-finger telling-off, the 'pull yourself together and just get on with being a mum' thing. If I could have got on with being a mum I would have, but I couldn't. I couldn't get out of bed in the morning or clean breakfast off my kitchen table – but I didn't know how to explain this to my doctor without feeling I was letting myself and my family down.

I took the 20mg tablets of Citalopram for a few weeks, and in truthfulness it wasn't much help. I'd been prepared for my symptoms to get worse before they got better, as I'd been warned by the doctor and in my thorough researching of the tablets online, but what I wasn't prepared for was the way they made me feel manic and paranoid, convinced that the whispered voices in my head were burglars or murderers threatening the safety of me and my children. I also wasn't prepared for the exhaustion the tablets caused, worse even than the sleepless nights I'd been experiencing with a newborn. Or the incessant chin tension they caused, meaning I'd grind my teeth constantly like a drug-addled maniac.

I returned to the doctor and told her that the sixteen hours a day of sleep the tablets were causing was unrealistic, especially for a mother of two kids under two who needed feeding, bathing and, most importantly, entertaining. She looked me up and down: 'You must be feeling better, you're not crying,' she said.

I nodded mutely, digested her advice to stop taking the tablets, listened while she told me that antidepressants only affected 10 per cent of your feelings anyway and believed her when she told me I'd be fine without any help. I was disheartened but so desperate to feel normal that I accepted what she'd said to me, returning to my house of misery. I hoped that if she told me enough times that I was going to be OK then I would be – that I'd be returned to my former self.

My life at that time felt like it was being lived through a sheet of glass. It was happening, I was looking at it, but in no way was I an active part of any of it. Sometimes the window would open a crack, allowing me to reach in and touch myself, be a present part of my family, but I was otherwise distanced, disengaged, going through the motions of my life and watching as if it were all happening to someone else.

In the weeks that followed I did the most important thing I could have ever done for my own recovery: I started talking about it. I blogged about the way I felt and chatted to other mums at the few baby groups I had the guts to attend. Through emails from friends and readers it slowly dawned on me that I didn't have to accept the paltry morsels of support my GP had thrown me; I deserved and needed more. It was not OK that my life was crap – it didn't have to be that way – but it was up to me to ask for help. And if this was going to happen, I had to speak to someone a bit more sympathetic to the needs of mothers. Which is why I called in the big guns: disregarding the fact my baby was probably too old for this, I plucked up my courage, hunted out Hux's red logbook and gave my health visitor a call.

She comes to see me the next morning and, though I believe I am presenting a pretty together version of myself, the concerned look on her face as she walks through the front door suggests otherwise. Will has worked from home to provide by his presence some familiarity and comfort, but I can tell he feels as clueless and confused as I do, seeing his wife and the mother of his children disintegrate before his eyes. I want to reassure him that I'm OK, I'm fine, we're all going to come out of this unscathed, but I can't, because I really don't know if we will. At that point I've started fantasising that maybe I'll get sent to a psychiatric ward for a bit; maybe I'll get to go away for a rest. I'm so exhausted that taking part in *Girl, Interrupted*: the live version seems like a viable and attractive option (though from what I've heard it's not as easy on the NHS; there's no crazy Angelina Jolie fighting for your friendship), an actual prison of a locked ward seems better than the pseudo-jail of my own home.

I try to meet the health visitor's gaze as Will hovers around the door between the living room and the kitchen, nervously enquiring whether anybody wants a cup of tea. I chit-chat about Huxley and bring up the topic of feeling 'a bit off' before bursting into hot and embarrassed tears.

'I don't know what to do,' I tell her between sniffly sobs. 'I've tried medication, I've tried going to the doctor, I've even tried going for a run! I just don't like my life.'

She becomes the second authority figure, after my friendly police officer, to sit on that sofa and sympathetically pat my hand.

'It doesn't have to be this way,' she affirms. 'You need to enjoy being a mother.'

In a move that I take to mean the situation in my head is pretty dire, she calls the doctor's surgery and insists an appointment – with a different GP – is released to me later that same day. On attendance I'm swiftly prescribed Prozac and given a referral to an urgent care mental health team, who assess me and diagnose me with severe post-natal depression and anxiety. Always the over-achiever . . . This is one situation where I would have been gladder not to score a full house.

They diagnose me by passing me a questionnaire to fill out that is classic NHS: it looks like it's been photocopied about a million times until the black ink has gone all grey and blotchy. I duly fill it out and am scored on a scale for depression and anxiety. For both I score eighteen, which means it's bloody serious – the highest score you can achieve (though I'm not sure 'achieve' is the right word in the context) is twenty-one and anything over sixteen is considered a serious case. I'm gutted to be officially certified bonkers but also feel some relief at the fact that my precarious mental state has been acknowledged, and for the first time I feel a real drive and possibility that I can get better and perhaps enjoy my life once more. Finally there is a light at the end of my mental health tunnel.

I don't know how I've arrived at the life I seem to be living. On the surface I have everything I've ever wanted – the husband, the suburban house, the kids. But inside I've never been more miserable.

One of my favourite books has always been the brilliant *Prozac Nation* by Elizabeth Wurtzel, and I feel some comfort in the fact that I'm sharing a medication with a woman I've always so admired. I take my pills daily and religiously, telling myself my mental illness errs on the side of tortured artist instead of crazy suburban mother. Slowly, slowly I start to feel better: reading between the lines of my frantic statements about family life and mental health, a friend sends me an envelope of seeds for the garden, telling me that digging in the soil will prove therapeutic. She's right; the hard weeding and planning of spring bulbs helps enormously – and turns out to be the final activity we will ever do as a family.

I sometimes wondered if Will's long hours at work had anything to do with my demise, whether things would have been different if he'd worked a 9–5 job locally rather than an eighty-hour week with too many overnights in London. I don't think that anything would have paused my journey to crazy-town; the experience I went through was going to happen whether I had one husband or six of them at home. You can't argue with brain chemicals: mine were skewed and Will could have done nothing to change that. On the contrary, had he lent more support I would have had more time to fester in bed, languish in my own feelings of self-pity, sleep my days away. Granted, he didn't understand what I was going through, believing I was lazy rather than ill. But had he been around a bit more I wouldn't have been so motivated to get help (and Prozac). I think he was almost as relieved as me to discover that I was going mad and wasn't just a bad mother. But that wasn't enough to save our marriage.

CHAPTER EIGHT

The City That Never Sleeps

Before long it's quite evident to both my husband and me that our marriage is going down the pan.

When people enquire about the reasons behind this marriage breakdown it's usually in the hushed, apologetic tones I imagine they otherwise reserve for complaining in restaurants or talking at funerals, as if they're embarrassed to be asking me why I was such a failure at my marriage. I never mind: I guess it's only natural to be inquisitive about someone's motivations to destroy their family, to so thoroughly change the course of their life. I feel judged but I try not to worry about those who have such obvious opinions when it comes to my failed marriage – I've definitely done the same to myself on more than one occasion, given myself a thorough bollocking for letting my whole family down.

I always believe people to be disappointed at the answer I give, because the truth is, I don't really know why it all went south so quickly. There was no watershed moment, no plates dramatically thrown at the walls. The police weren't involved as we screamed obscenities at each other and there were no long or agonisingly drawn-out, emotionally charged conversations in front of a couples counsellor. Perhaps our split would have been easier and happened quicker if there were?

Quite simply, we fell out of love.

Will and I met when we were very young. I was a baby at eighteen, he a slightly more grown-up twenty-one. We grew through our early twenties together, marrying young, having children young and settling down young; it's difficult to start a family and raise children when you're still a child yourself, not knowing who you are or where you want to go in life, and we were no exception to this rule.

Towards the end of our relationship we talked sometimes about whether our marriage was destined to fail – that is, when we were talking at all – and one evening in the midst of my post-natal Prozac fug, Will came home and told me he was going away for a week to think over our relationship.

I remember thinking at the time that his being away wasn't going to make much of a difference as he spent much of his week away at work anyway, and so with a vow to give him space as he moved in with his business partner for a week, I stepped back and got on with life as I knew it: being Mum, trying to be less mental, working hard to get out of bed in the morning.

On his return he suggested I might like to do the same. He noted that I'd been under some pressure (going completely mad with two children under two and a husband who stayed away as often as possible? DEFINITE PRESSURE, DUDE), and asked if I thought I might go to stay with friends in London or perhaps Nottingham, the city we'd just moved from. I rolled my eyes and, in a fit of what was back then uncharacteristic defiance and confidence, texted my friend Kate in New York to tell her my marriage was circling the drain and did she fancy a transatlantic visitor for a week so I could mull the whole situation over?

As a family we weren't flush with cash at that time, but after completing a couple of work projects I had about a thousand quid in the bank and couldn't think of any way I'd rather spend it: on myself in NYC. I booked my flights that very same night and tried to get my head around taking a week away from my children.

The persistent feeling of guilt so many of us experience is quite unique to motherhood. It pursues us *constantly*: we feel guilty for being a working mum, for not being a working mum. Feel guilty for co-sleeping, using a cot. Feel guilty for being a free-range parent or following the Gina Ford method. Guilt is everywhere and it never leaves as we fight to work out how we can possibly make the best decisions for our kids all the freaking time. It's why so many of us look five years older than we are and why you could plant sunflowers in the furrows on our foreheads.

This week's guilt came from leaving my children. Hux wasn't even one and Elfie just two years old – how could I even think to leave them? I had breasts that were still dripping milk and the fact I'd be taking my mammaries a whole ocean away made me quiver with worry – though, it has to be said, a little bit of excitement too.

Kate completely came through for me on the supportive friend front and called me the day before my flight to deliver some good news. With Will away once more, I'd gathered the strength to take the children to a local village fete and I took the call with a half-eaten child-sized ice cream in one hand, watching my toddler play on a bouncy castle. Kate told me she'd upgraded me with her points to business class, a treat I would never have even dreamed of in my deepest darkest days of sleep deprivation. Not only would I get to sleep on the plane, but I'd get to do it on an actual bed and with a bellyful of free champagne: as someone who relished the silence on a train ride sans kids this didn't just sound like heaven, this sounded like the absolute pinnacle of my life. And that was affirmed on the way over to JFK as I sat in my seat that was bigger than any other I'd ever seen on an aeroplane and thought, you know what, if this vessel goes down today I will die happy. God bless that bottomless booze the cabin crew insisted on bringing to me: it was like Faliraki 2003 but with a bit more class and a lot fewer fishbowls.

The thrill of autonomous travel and excitement of being out of the house unladen with small people and their associated paraphernalia had me giddy, almost drunk with possibility as well as champagne. On landing in the city I shot into Williamsburg in a yellow taxi (SQUEAL! Just like in the movies!) to drop off my bags and head straight back out again to the Commodore, a southern-style bar on Metropolitan Avenue, for fried chicken and Southern biscuits – whatever they were.

New York City is so special. Believe everything you see on *Sex and the City*; it's all true (apart from all the eye-rolling crap about men – don't believe that nonsense). The city has a special pulse that I've never felt anywhere else in the world before or since, and is full of the most incredible spots to discover. I'd only ever been once before as a wide-eyed twenty-one-year-old tourist with my then-husband-to-be, but this trip as a solo explorer felt completely different; lacking a man at my side and spending my days wandering the city as Kate worked, I saw the place with completely new eyes and allowed myself to take it all in.

On my first full day in New York I visit the *VICE* offices in Brooklyn, the outpost of the company I used to work for back in London. Touring the office, I hug the ex-colleagues who have since moved over here to have their own American adventures, swapping stories with my old CEO and feeling jealous of the team members I once employed who have accelerated past me in their careers, leaving me behind in a cloud of dust and babies. I'm happy for them, of course, but I can't help but feel a pang of 'What if?' as I look around at the new lives they've bravely embarked on. Could this have been mine, I wonder, if I hadn't got pregnant? If I hadn't become so reliant on a man – my husband – would I also be living this Carrie Bradshaw life in New York City?

At one point I catch sight of something completely unexpected that makes my breath catch in my chest. In a corridor just outside one of the editing suites is a wall of staff photos, a record of Polaroids with scribbled notes from happy and relaxed-looking employees, goofily posing with thumbs up or laughing heartily with their heads thrown back. I smile in familiarity as I notice a couple of my old London colleagues – and then am stopped dead in my tracks when my eye catches my own smile staring back at me.

There I am, sitting back in my old chair at my old desk in my old office on Leonard Street, cheesily grinning for the camera with one hand on my laptop and the other raised in a wave. Embarrassingly, a tear springs to my eye as I feel huge nostalgia for that life I used to have and so readily said goodbye to, the one where I had a professional purpose, a budget, a life. It's a stark reminder of who I used to be and I feel so sad at the contrast of who I am now in comparison.

Waving goodbye to my old friends, I head to another bar with Kate for yet another cocktail, and I promise myself I can be that person again.

The innocuous moment when I realise my marriage is over; I'm in the Mexican restaurant La Superior on South Second and Berry. I sit drinking margaritas and eating chips and dip with Kate and a couple of old work friends, gleefully clapping along as a mariachi band plays while strolling around us, Mexican guitar players with the most incredible handlebar moustaches strumming along to the accompanying trumpets and violins. In a sudden, unexpected moment I feel so exhilarated and thrilled, a rush of possibility and peace coming over me simultaneously. Rarely in the last three years have I let myself feel this pure unadulterated happiness that I'm experiencing now, this pleasure to just *live*. I've let go of the worries and the headaches of my marriage and am finding joy in the possibility of being me. And that feels like something I'm going to want to feel again.

Before New York I'd never spent more than forty-eight hours away from my children. It was on a work retreat when Hux was six months old, and the guilt I felt over the trip was only soothed by the fact that I had been so exhausted I had barely been able to keep my eyes open long enough to drive there. It had been fun but I'd revelled in early nights and long bathtimes rather than tons of socialising with the other delegates, retreating to the bathroom eight times a day to pump my rock-solid breasts that painfully missed their intended, worrying my son would be missing my comfort as he drank the milk I'd spent the previous month expressing for him out of cold, plastic bottles.

But this time I had vowed not to feel guilt or worry for being away from my children, something much easier said than done given their tender young ages and the fact that we were rarely separated. I tried to keep from FaceTiming them too often, calling only twice during my trip, as each call finished with my having a little lonely cry because my heart felt empty at the sight of their beautiful faces that I was so far away from. Drying my tears, I would tell myself I was doing the right thing; I needed this time to rediscover the essence of myself and work out what I truly wanted out of life, whether that was my husband or not.

The remainder of my week in New York went by in a whirlwind of sightseeing, cocktails and burgers, my heart expanding for the new city I was coming to know almost as much as it had expanded when I met my children.

I sit on the shore of the East River to the side of Smorgasburg, the weekly Brooklyn food market, surveying Manhattan and reviewing my life. With a snap I realise I don't feel sad any more and, while in America, haven't spent one second struggling to see a purpose to my life. I guiltily think of the Prozac I'd accidentally left at home, half hidden in the cupboard above the kettle next to the tea caddy and my favourite mug, and realise I haven't missed my antidepressants. I haven't felt one withdrawal symptom at all and, though I know I shouldn't simply come off medication without the advice of a doctor, I make a vow that I will never take one of those little blue tablets ever again. I will – I know I can – find happiness in myself.

CHAPTER NINE

How to Split Up With Your Husband

Out of all my recently discovered middle-class problems, one of the most harrowing is how difficult the red-eye from New York to London is. Disregarding its sinister name, I had always thought this flight would be a rather pleasant way to travel: you hop on a plane in the Big Apple in the evening, fly through the night and wake up six hours later in London. Very civilised, very sophisticated.

In reality it's not that way at all. Having travelled over the Atlantic in business class, I was disappointed to find that I'd reach nowhere close to the comfort levels of my previous journey's flat bed and on-board bar as I travelled home. On boarding the aircraft I turned right but wistfully looked left, already missing the crisp duvet and even crisper Sauvignon Blanc of the previous journey. I took my seat next to an eighty-year-old man who, over the next six hours, would give me a run-down of each and every one of his grand- and great-grandkids.

I was at least on the way home, though, and by now I was missing my children with a physical ache: I couldn't wait to land at Heathrow so I could get home and see them again.

But first, that uncomfortable flight. Soon after take-off, dinner was thrown at me by a grumpy member of the cabin crew, along with a couple of mini bottles of wine to help soothe me into the land of nod. Wanting to get to sleep fast so I wouldn't be a mardy bastard the next day – I find it physically impossible to do anything but growl in response to anyone trying to talk to me pre-9 a.m. on the best of days, so goodness knew how I'd feel with jetlag – I wildly scrabbled to eat as fast as possible. I soon realised that on the red-eye any kind of sleep is pretty much an impossibility as it was only 8 p.m., my bedroom was a metal tube smelling of other people's farts and school dinners and I was surrounded by 200 strangers. Civilised and sophisticated my arse.

In my bed of an upright seat with a 30-inch pitch I spent the night feeling so confined I couldn't even toss and turn, and every time I managed to drop off I jolted awake again, consumed by thoughts about my children in between ponderings on whether or not my scratchy blanket had been laundered before it was handed to me by the cabin crew (googling says most likely not. Gross).

I finished the flight eating rubbery scrambled eggs with a plastic fork, almost delirious with tiredness and time-zone confusion, landing in what was the middle of the night in my originating country and feeling as disoriented as if I'd spent the entire time awake. Which I had.

We landed and I contemplated getting a coffee; I felt tired enough that I could have lain down in the middle of the arrivals hall and fallen dead asleep, right in the midst of the Heathrow bustle. But I figured that caffeine would do nothing but turn me into more of a jittery mess than I was before (I was missing those children so much it was making me shake) and I didn't want to mess up my bedtime patterns for the foreseeable future. So I kept planting one foot in front of the other in search of the M25 and my route home.

It was in this knackered and wired state that I hopped in the car back to my husband from my formative trip to New York to end my marriage.

On that flight my mind had been turning as much as my body, a weird mix of foreboding and excitement mingling with the plane food in my belly. On our descent into Heathrow I'd dug into the interior pocket of my handbag – the cavernous one that ironically doubled up as a nappy bag when I was in my usual role of devoted mother to Elfie and Hux – to find the wedding and engagement rings I had experimentally and temporarily removed five days previous. Though my finger had felt weirdly light, I hadn't missed them as I thought I would, and as I replaced them on the fourth finger of my left hand I wondered how long they'd remain.

I often think of that moment on the plane when I'm people-watching and considering other people's busy lives. There I was, a solo GAP-clad, tanned and seemingly happy twenty-seven-year-old on a transatlantic flight. To an outside observer I might have appeared to be returning from a couple of days' work, a long weekend's shopping or even a little later-life travelling. I don't expect anyone on that flight would have looked at me and thought, 'WOAH! That woman's about to end her marriage!'

Yet I was.

*   *   *

My mother picks me up from the airport and the subject of my precarious relationship is the elephant in the room (the elephant in the car?), the chasm that feels as wide as the Atlantic I'd just crossed. Never a morning person and even less so after crossing five time zones overnight, I don't feel like talking beyond the superlatives I use to describe the top-level overview of the trip: Brooklyn, friends, flea markets, rooftop cocktails, Mexican food, oh my!

We drive home mostly in friendly silence, interspersed with catching up on the home gossip of my short week away, the minutiae of the latest village drama.

Arriving at my house, I am ecstatic at the touch and smell of my children, hugging them to me like my life depends on it. If sniffing the scent of the tops of their heads was a competitive sport I'd be winning gold right now. We cuddle on the sofa with my nose nestled in their deliciously downy scalps.

At barely six and twenty-eight months they have no idea their parents are about to turn their worlds upside down and I don't really know what to do with that feeling. I have butterflies in my stomach, as if I'm about to move house or go to university; my butterflies know that big changes are on the horizon but they're not quite sure where or in what direction. Like me they're slightly lost, directionless, aware this change has to be made but not sure what the outcome will be. I wish someone would tell me what I should do.

Knowing the full scale of the conversation I'm about to have with my husband, my mother returns to pick up the children for a playdate, leaving the house empty of kids yet full to bursting with expectation.

I sit on my bed, the bed I share with Will, and take a deep breath. My fully packed suitcase is still in the corner of the room, my handbag resting on top of it. I can see my folder of travel documents – flight confirmations, medical insurance documents – poking out of the opening. It might be the most turbulent time of my life but I'll never not be organised, will never risk a missed flight or holiday medical expense.

I lie down on top of my duvet, bury my face in the pillow I haven't seen for a week. This bed has been with us through cities and tragedies; it's seen the birth of two children and the death of one parent. It carries our scent, it holds our memories. In its headboard you can see the chips of too many careless removal men and the mattress is stained with the leaking breast milk that fed both of our babies, but it is us, it is ours, and I know I will miss it.

I feel sad.

I plod down the stairs towards the man who will be my husband for only a little time longer. There's so much we need to talk about but so little to say. We stand opposite each other at the kitchen counter, which gleams with a cleanliness that, given my New York absence, must be down to my mother-in-law.

'So,' he says.

'So,' I say.

'Do you want to start?' he asks. I really don't, but I will.

'I think we know it's over,' I tell him with a finality I'm not sure I feel.

'I think we do,' he agrees.

That's it. It's done. Marriage over. As simple as that.

All of a sudden, we begin to laugh. The situation we've found ourselves in is so ridiculous, so completely foreign, incredibly unexpected. How did we get here?

Will-and-Alice. Alice-and-Will. Our names always went together, like Ben & Jerry or Laurel and Hardy. Romeo and Juliet. I didn't know any different. I'd never wanted to.

He and I, who were termed 'the power couple' by piss-taking friends back in London, the twosome that was surely destined to be for ever. Ours was the best love story we knew; we were love's young dream. And, outside of Shakespearean tragedies, love's young dream isn't supposed to end.

I think back to when we first met. It was a Thursday night and, despite being tipsy at 4 a.m. on supermarket-brand vodka and Coke classily necked in the kitchen of my halls of residence, I remember it clearly: I'd been on two dates with JJ, a friend from the nightclub Will worked in, and had showed up after his shift at the club for a nightcap. As I was waiting outside the office for JJ, Will had appeared.

'You must be JJ's new girlfriend,' he said to me as I loitered awkwardly. We shook hands and I blushed: I'd moved to Nottingham only four months before and still felt like the adolescent country girl masquerading as someone confident enough to meet handsome men in the middle of the night for drinks.

The corridor smelled like stale beer and fag ash – back then weekends would be spent legally and accidentally getting burned by errant cigarette ends brandished by drunken dancers in clubs and bars. Smoking didn't kill you in those days – it was exotic, what the cool kids did, a chance to chat to the object of your affection under the literal smokescreen of asking for a light. And knowing I was in a club after dark to see a man when all the punters had gone home made me feel edgy, like I should probably take up the smoking I could smell all around me.

'We're just friends,' I hurriedly corrected him.

He nodded, raised his eyebrows and looked at me in a friendly way. 'This might sound like a weird question, but do you want a job?' he asked. 'We're opening a new nightclub and we need staff. I'd love for you to work there.'

I didn't want a job, not really. At school, I'd spent my weekends working for money to blow at Topshop, saving a tiny bit for uni, and having my parents cover my halls of residence rent and food made me feel rich when the bounty of my student loan appeared: I needed no more money to buy beer, books or jeans.

'Definitely!' I said. 'That would be great!'

Three days later I received a call to my newly purchased student-tariff mobile from an unknown number. I considered leaving it, not wanting to answer the phone to someone I didn't know – or worse, the bank enquiring about my rapidly increasing overdraft – but on an impulse picked up just before it went to voicemail. It was Will, inviting me to meet him for an interview.

I showed up at my allotted time wearing a beige duster jacket from French Connection that I still wear today – a bargain I'd picked up on a shopping trip with my mum at Bicester Shopping Village – a pair of indigo Diesel jeans and the only top I owned that made me look like I had something of a cleavage. I liked him and wanted to impress him but I wasn't sure why.

I sat opposite him as he spent five tentative minutes asking about my university course. I remember his hands trembling with nerves, which I thought was weird for an interviewer, as he asked me what bar experience I had (none), whether or not I liked dance music (nope) and what I wanted to do when I left uni (I had no idea). He told me where and when to come back for the induction. I felt a little annoyed that I'd got myself a job I didn't need, but subdued it with the thought that I'd be able to visit H&M as much as I wanted without depleting my loan or running up that overdraft.

At our induction we were given our uniform of black shirts from Zara, a company handbook and a crash course on being cool. The club was heavily dance-music based, something I truly didn't (and still don't) care much for, and I shrugged in ignorance as I was told about the opening weekend's headliners of Mr Scruff, Queens of Noize, Lee Burridge and Craig Richards – people who, in the coming years, I'd come to call pals. The musos around the room nodded in wide-eyed reverence as I giggled with Susie, a blonde-haired fellow new recruit who would be the very first person I told about my liaison with my new boss.

'Check him out,' she said, nodding towards dreamboat JJ. 'I fancy a bit of that!'

'Already have,' I nonchalantly told her, leading her to believe we'd 'done it', although we very much hadn't; it was an act that was still in those heady late-teenage days A Very Big Deal. And as JJ was the deputy manager of the new club we'd scored ourselves jobs at, that made lil' old provincial me feel particularly cool.

'You have him, I'll have the other one,' she said, nodding at JJ and then pointing at Will.

Of course, neither of us knew back then that the man she had designs on would come to be the father of my children, but I was increasingly intrigued by him. Before long, JJ was forgotten.

I worked for Will for an electric-charged five weeks before anything happened. As the manager of the club where I was bar staff, any liaisons between him and me were strictly forbidden, but he always gave me the best jobs, never stationing me in the dreaded cloakroom to swap numbered tickets for jackets and sweaty pound coins. I became the unofficial supervisor of the VIP bar, a job, he told me with a wink, he only let the prettiest girls do.

For someone who had no interest in working in a nightclub I was having a pretty brilliant time.

The night we had our first kiss was actually the morning after. The club was Nottingham's latest-opening venue, not shutting its doors to the crowds of hardened music fans until 6 a.m., and though this was a time I'd only ever previously seen when getting up early for flights, I always tagged along for post-work wind-down drinks. As a hormone-driven student, I wasn't going to say no to a couple of bottles of Beck's and the chance to flirt with my boss.

That morning of our first tryst followed a busy night at the club and found the night's bar staff sitting on the stage in the main room of the club downstairs, laughing about the punters who'd been in on that shift. Will and I had already found our mutual connection – we'd grown up just a few miles away from one another – and that morning that tenuous commonality was our excuse to stay glued together.

A couple of hours in and things were starting to get merry. The club opening had been a tough time for everyone, with us all wanting to impress and work hard. Will in particular was pulling eighty-hour weeks and by that point thoroughly needed to let his hair down. The Beck's and the mindless chatter of a group of work friends who just wanted to get pissed and have a laugh was enough for him to relax, and before I knew it his head was reclining in my lap.

Unaccustomed to such overt displays of affection, I wasn't sure what to do. My prior romantic experience was mostly limited to snogs with boys in dark bars or the couple of 'serious' (read: totally innocent) boyfriends I'd met through friends, and I'd only been on a couple of juvenile dates to the cinema or the local bowling alley. I was taken aback, but though the feeling was foreign I went with it and tentatively stroked his hair. He didn't demur, and though the other staff members must have been aware of our displays of affection they were either too drunk or didn't care enough to say anything. Even George, the owner of the venue, turned a blind eye to our relationship, both then and in the following months.

'Don't poke the payroll!' he'd chortle at us with a wink and a nudge when he caught us sneaking a kiss in the reception booth.

The staff party soon dissipated, and Will offered the war cry of 'All back to mine!' to nobody in particular. But by now it was nine on a Sunday morning and tiredness was kicking in: people were dropping like flies, flies who'd been working behind a sticky bar for the last eight hours. Not me though; invigorated with a rush of attraction and adrenaline, I accompanied Will home with my co-bar worker Craig, a music studies student who held the new object of my affection in revered high esteem.

When we arrived back at Will's city centre pad that he shared with a couple of mates, a DJ and a music producer, I was totally in awe of the coolness of it all. It wasn't well-decorated or at all clean, but it was a new build apartment with an open-plan kitchen and featured a double-height living space where Will's mezzanine-level bedroom was housed. The furniture was cobbled together: a hand-me-down sofa paired with a saggy futon, an IKEA coffee table strewn with club flyers and tobacco; but compared to my out-of-town single-bed student room with its plastic-covered mattress and fluorescent-lit kitchen it was a veritable palace – and one I'd be living in within six weeks.

Will poured us drinks and we sat on the sofa with Craig, the ultimate third wheel, wedged between us.

He and I looked at each other. We each knew what the other wanted. In my eighteen years I'd never felt an attraction like it: I wanted him, and the fact that we had a rabbiting gooseberry in our way made me long for him even more. We indulged Craig, letting him pick Will's brains on the subject of all the DJs he'd ever met as we plied him with booze, and soon that had the desired effect. Our gooseberry was asleep.

After carrying on the small talk facade for only moments longer, Will and I kissed.

It was magical.

Our magic remained for a long time. Up until our relationship went south, Will was always incredibly kind, thoughtful and considerate towards me. He cared as deeply for me and I did him, and our odd and offbeat senses of humour meshed well, meaning we spent most of our time together in stitches. Our formative years were spent together and we truly grew up as a couple, happily finding our feet in so many ways in our twosome. Early on I knew I wanted to be with him for ever: we spoke about marriage from the beginning and I could never see myself with anyone else.

I would come to wonder if our extreme closeness was in part to blame for our demise. I had never been independent and away from my parents save for the few months I spent in student accommodation, and the way Will and I grew together meant I saw him as an appendage to me, an arm or a foot. I stopped looking on him as an individual, someone to be considered and not taken for granted; we were never independent of each other and I didn't consider him as a separate person with differing thoughts, feelings and opinions to me, not as I should have.

That night of the staff party was also the first time we made love, more than once, high up in his mezzanine bedroom while Craig slept on the sofa. We continued into the next day long after Craig went home, as his flatmates busied themselves down below, watching TV and hoovering. We didn't care. We couldn't get enough of each other.

That weekend time stood still. It was a bank holiday and the first night Will had taken off since the club opened. We spent the entire time together, with me only going home after two nights so that I could pick up clean knickers and use my own razor. On our third consecutive evening glued at the hip I met his sister, who was in town to visit friends, and we cemented our relationship that evening sharing our life stories and a kebab on a step outside a shop closed for the break.

Will and I moved in together after six weeks and were engaged (and deliriously happy) six months after that.

Our relationship was led by our hearts, our hormones and our crotches; we craved each other with a ferocity I'd never felt before in my short life. I remember, leaving Will to visit my parents six weeks after our getting together, sobbing at our goodbye, feeling a physical sense of being bereft at the thought of a weekend apart. For him I felt lovesick: he had become not just a partner but a part of me, undetachable, an intrinsic fragment of my being. I was him and he was me: we were one.

But stood across from each other in our 2013 kitchen, miles and years away from that 6 a.m. club in 2004 Nottingham, we weren't one any more. We weren't Will-and-Alice.

We were Will. And Alice. Separate. Separated.

'Shall we take our rings off?' I asked with some nervous laughter. And we do.

Nobody talks about what you should do with your wedding bands when you remove them. My engagement ring was the most special piece of jewellery I'd ever owned: a carat-sized solitaire diamond perched atop a platinum ring, it was, outside of my family, what I treasured most. I'd worn that ring for almost ten years and hated to remove it, but it symbolised something that in that moment was so broken I was almost happy to see my naked finger underneath.

That ring would live in a box in my wardrobe for the next three years. I tried to sell it on a couple of occasions, but second-hand diamonds aren't as lucrative as you'd imagine, and I decided to save it in case my daughter ever wanted a keepsake of her parents' fractured partnership.

Now, almost five years on, as a single woman I'm happy to wear it on my right hand on special occasions. It no longer reflects a couple who unexpectedly drifted in opposite directions, but a time in my life when I was so deliriously happy I wanted to be tied to a man, my best friend, for the rest of my life. It reflects the love we shared that at one point was so huge we moved cross-country together, we went through the death of a parent together, we sat and held hands over our dangerously ill daughter together. It represents a partnership that gave me the two most beautiful children I've ever seen and that is something to be immensely proud of.

That's the perspective that time and distance gives you. No longer do you feel anger over what someone else might have done or said; you feel thankful for what went before. You might be strangers now – we certainly were – but a shared history of love, tenderness and family will always remain.

It might not have been for ever but at that time it was very right.

Our split felt like a weird one and in most ways seemed altogether completely different to what I had expected: on removing the rings I instantly felt free, like my clipped wings had repaired themselves and the world was at my feet. I felt an urge to do things for the first time in years: calling on babysitters to go to the pub with friends, without asking permission from my hard-working husband. I felt liberated and had no trouble with finding support and help in family and friends eager to assist the newly single mum. I suspected that they felt sorry for me but I didn't care; having felt like I hadn't thought of my own happiness for weeks and months, I was happy to indulge a couple of baby-free whims for once.

Will and I had got together when I was fresh out of my parents' house, and the thought of an independent life simultaneously terrified and excited me. I might not have known who our energy provider was or quite when the bins went out and I may have suddenly had two children under two to support on no income, but I felt that the world was my optimistic oyster.

When my husband came home that fateful evening to suggest I take a couple of days to get my head together before we made any big decisions, booking myself a flight to New York was the last thing he would have expected me to do. I wouldn't have thought it of myself either, but I did it on a wonderful urge, and though I didn't know it at the time it was a decision that would change my life, the very first step I took to reclaiming myself.

I expected to jet out to JFK a quivering mess, spend my holiday time questioning how I could possibly leave my babies for nigh on a week and return home the same emotionally frail weeper who left London.

But what happened instead was that, in deciding to end my marriage on that trip, I also rediscovered my spark, somehow uncovering the essence of who I was (or who I once had been), seemingly buried underneath a heap of NYC cheeseburgers and margaritas. I suddenly felt ten years younger and ten pounds lighter, despite the junk food: I was confident, happy, sprightly. The distance allowed me to gain the perspective I needed to evaluate where I was in my life and the direction I wanted to go in – the opposite of the path I was currently on.

Of course I was heartbroken to say goodbye to the man I loved and would grieve the loss of my marriage and my family beyond expectation, but the happiness I felt at welcoming back the person I loved even more – myself – was indescribable.

And this is something that resonates even now, five years into a single life with a raft of relationships under my belt. I've dated a couple of people for extended periods in this time, and if ever I'm unsure about where I'm going there's a mantra I like to consider: 'I like you, but I love me more.'

With this mantra you will never be unhappy in a relationship, because it means you refuse to let another person put their own happiness above your own. You may truly love the one you're with and that goes a long way when it comes to compromise and sacrifice, but in my experience unless you truly love and cherish yourself you won't be able to find ultimate contentment.

I like you – but I love me more.

I was alone.

CHAPTER TEN

Work That Works

This may well be stating the bloody obvious but it's really hard to split up with the person you believed you'd spend your life with. Prior to my divorce, if you'd asked me what was my biggest challenge I would have said long division, but the logistics of a life alone with two children was a whole other maths problem.

Diary management aside, I found the whole nightmare of having to adjust my mind's expectations for the rest of my life the hardest thing of all: throughout my adolescence I'd become so attuned to the expectation of my future marriage and children that having to wave goodbye to a situation that was so intrinsically part of my 'Big Life Plan' was incredibly difficult.

Though I'd been lucky enough never to experience the death of a loved one, I likened my divorce to a bereavement, going through the motions as people do when they lose someone close to them. I felt like the main driver behind my divorce had been the changes Will and I had gone through in the last few years, the fact that we'd been so young when we'd met each other and had been through an incredibly formative time – our tempestuous early twenties – as a couple. Post-split I looked around me and it made so much sense; my closest friends had spent this period of their lives working on their careers, going wild in big cities and waking up in strangers' beds, not saying 'I do', giving birth and moving to the suburbs. Will and I were babies when we met and still had so much growing we needed to do that it's no wonder we did so in totally opposite directions.

Despite the fact that I knew the split had to happen, I felt totally winded and gutted – what an understatement – by the whole divorce fandango. Aside from the fear of being alone I had absolutely no idea how to make ends meet. Or how on earth I'd retain my sanity, waking up day after day to deal with two children alone. Or even what my friends and neighbours would think of me, a single mum at the age of twenty-seven: would I become some sort of stereotype, claiming benefits and doing nothing but watch daytime TV, stagnating in my standstill life until my kids were old enough to fly the nest? Would I wake up one morning on the *Jeremy Kyle* set having a DNA test? I didn't know who I was without my husband by my side, and I was terrified that that person would turn out to be some kind of benefits scrounger, demoted to the lowest echelons of society.

I panicked. I didn't know how I'd make ends meet, either emotionally or financially. I didn't want to be a solo parent; I never asked to be the one responsible for raising two children. It wasn't the life I expected. I wasn't even brave enough to sleep properly when Will wasn't at home: how on earth would I forge a life without him?

My husband left our home and went to stay with his mum for a while, a short mile away. He'd spend a couple of evenings a week with the children and I'd vacate the house so he could be alone with them. Occasionally he would stay over: with both children having their own bedroom we didn't have one spare, so he was forced to awkwardly return to the marital bed on these occasions. We'd spend the night perched on the edge of our respective sides of the mattress, building a pillow fort between us lest we accidentally touch in the middle of the night. Looking back at the entirety of our union, piling IKEA pillows in the middle of our bed to make sure we had no contact was a definite low point.

Over a couple of weeks we discussed our children and their future arrangements and I quickly realised I wasn't going to get what I wanted out of our custody deliberations. Still feeling delicate from the madness induced by my post-natal depression and not even sure I should be left with such a big responsibility as solo parenting, I didn't want to give up the support I felt I needed at home to successfully bring up two children: I worried the pressure of doing this alone would send me right back to bonkersville . . . do not pass go, do not collect £200. A game of Monopoly that I couldn't even cheat at.

But he felt that, having moved out to where we lived in Buckinghamshire so I could be close to my parents, there was nothing left for him in this area. 'I never wanted to move to Milton Keynes,' he said to me, on one of the long and arduous evenings that saw us debating his living situation.

'Neither did I!' I replied.

Will wanted to be back in London to pursue his career without the pressure of an hour-long commute daily, and so that's what he did.

I wish I could have said to this, 'Fair enough, we do what we think is right,' but I couldn't. I was fuming. I didn't want the father of my children living fifty miles down the M1, seeing them every other weekend and some holidays. I wanted him close by, sharing the responsibility of the children – and their PND-mental mother – as I felt he should and I needed. I didn't make the decision to have them on my own, so why should I be left literally holding the babies?

But he wouldn't budge and that was that. I was all alone. Me, a nine-month-old and a newly two-year-old, all alone in our house. With no job and what felt like no hope. Fucking great.

I did what the internet told me at this point and googled the benefits I'd be entitled to, filling in a long form that would allow me to claim tax credits. Will arranged for me to have a modest amount from him monthly and, the resulting amount not being enough for the three of us to live off, I pondered what I could do to raise the rest of our living expenses. For a while I was despondent, certain I'd be hunting down more benefits and selling off my belongings to raise funds before I knew it. I started listing old clothes and baby items on eBay, looking at ways to raise some much-needed cash.

Until, quite unexpectedly, something switched in me. I woke up one morning and didn't roll back over with the pillow over my head, as I usually did, wanting anything but to get up and face the day. Instead I sat up and placed my feet on the ground with an intention that I hadn't felt previously, opened the curtains and felt like a human who wanted to partake in life.

I don't know where it came from, but I suddenly knew that I wasn't going to be a single-mum sad case who plodded along on a teeny-tiny income; I wasn't going to flounder and beg my parents or ex-husband for help. I was going to do this independent life thing and by God I was going to do it properly.

That day Will and I had one of our first terrible post-split arguments. Fuelled by a sense of injustice and my tiger mother instincts, I screamed at him, asking how he dared leave his family in the lurch like this, buggering back off to his life in London as if the last three years hadn't happened. I told him that I, we, didn't need him, that we didn't want him, that I could raise this family all on my own without his help. I shouted that I didn't want his money, that I was going to get myself to a place where I could support my children on my own without taking his handouts. I was going to be a success for my children, I knew it.

Of course, six months down the line when I realised there was no shame in taking bloody child maintenance from my kids' father, I quickly retracted the statement, chuckling to Will when he hopefully asked if I wanted him to stop paying me money now I was all independent and things.

Though the children were so young, the hardest thing about our split was seeing how it affected them. Hux wasn't able to verbalise his thoughts and feelings but Elfie became very confused, asking where Daddy was and saying how sad she was that he wasn't at home. It was awful and I know everyone found these early parts of the split hard, Will because he was away from the children and I because the emotions and questions were difficult to field alone when I didn't know the correct answers.

It wasn't all bad, though. We both spent more quality time with the children, going to toddler groups, crafting, cooing, visiting playgrounds. The fact that their dad was away most of the time made me want to make sure that when we were together our time was happy and full of joy, so we left the house a lot more than we had done before. Despite my family life having evaporated before my eyes I'd suddenly become the mum I had always wanted to be: one who crafts, cooks, goes to bloody baby groups. They loved it and, though I was hesitant to admit it, I kind of loved it too.

Solo parenting brought with it a whole host of new skills I needed to learn in the form of around-the-house jobs. Having spent my entire adult life living with a man and relying on him for 'boy jobs', it was a big shock to realise I'd have to deal with stuff like bin juice and BBQs on my own.

The first time someone came round to read the meter I looked at him blankly and asked him what a meter looked like. The first time I tried to mow the lawn I did it in flip-flops and mowed straight over the power cord, causing the entire house's fuse box to trip (finding that on my own was fun, too). The first time I had to remove a large spider from the bath on my own I almost had an aneurysm. You could say that becoming the matriarch of the family was a learning curve: I bet Kris Jenner has someone who'll remove spiders for her.

Will had left me with a few things: two lovely children, a three-bedroomed rented house in an expensive Buckinghamshire village and a car that leaked so much there was mould on the passenger door. The driver's side window on that bloody car no longer worked, either – try managing your order when you're going through the McDonald's drive-thru (as you do plenty when you're a single mother who's so sleep-deprived you can barely wipe your own bum, let alone cook seven healthy lunches and dinners every week).

I decided to divide and conquer and worked out how I could solve my problems one by one, as quickly and effectively as possible.

First off, the car. My parents offered to lend me some money so I could purchase one that felt like slightly less of a death trap and, though I was hesitant to take cash off anyone, I accepted £5,000 and bought a used – and, crucially, watertight and working – Ford Focus. Sorted.

Second was the house. Though it was in a lovely spot and in a lovely village it was very expensive for what it was, and in a location that was totally geared towards families. Since mine and Will's split I'd uncomfortably noticed the way that local women acquaintances had started treating me differently, looking me with a hesitance and suspicion that I hadn't noticed before. They were clearly uncomfortable in my presence, especially if their husbands were in the vicinity, and I deduced they were worried that now I was down one husband I was after theirs.

I was desperate to laugh every time I felt this odd atmosphere around these people. 'I can't even handle my own husband!' I wanted to say to them. 'What would make you think I could handle yours, too?!'

And so I moved out of the pretty village and into the slightly less attractive town of Milton Keynes, a place that has won no awards for its stark concrete aesthetic but would prove convenient in its proximity to places that would allow me to have something of a – gasp – solo social life.

Next up was the money thing. Ah, the money thing. Quite

crucial, the money, when you're trying to raise a family and do fun things like feed, clothe and educate them.

I'd kept my blog ticking over while giving birth to Hux and it had proved an essential outlet when writing about my post-natal depression and marriage breakdown. Writing had been something of a therapy to me in the old LiveJournal days, a way I processed situations, thoughts and feelings. I needed that like some people need to run a 10k to get over a bad day.

My blog, and later Instagram account, also had the benefit of connecting me to a huge network of women (and some men) who'd been through similar to me. Their support and help through this time was invaluable and I think I would have been a much less sane person without it.

After writing for some time about my experiences I started to hear more and more from people all over the world who had been through, or were about to go through, the process of separation or divorce. To this day this remains one of the most valuable parts of my job, the networks I form and people who reach out to me. It's so important to me that my words are helpful to others and really, I'm not sure I'd do my job if writing about my experiences didn't plainly help both women and men who are going through such a turbulent time in their lives. When Will and I started talking about divorce and separation the only materials I found to read were from my doctor or government-sponsored websites; what I could have done with at the time was real human reassurance that everything was going to be OK, and this is what I hope I offer to others in a time and situation where everything can seem so hopeless.

As well as being my therapy and a resource for others, my blog was a modest money-spinner. When Will left it was bringing in around £600 a month and I thought that, with my marketing background and drive to succeed, I could surely elevate this to more. And so I started working on regular content, being more thoughtful about the time and work I put into the website. It quickly flourished and its income started to grow.

Though I had a fairly solid base level of income now, I knew if I worked a little bit harder I could bring in more money. And so I launched a small one-woman (I called it 'boutique') marketing consultancy, working with small enterprises to develop their online business and communications strategies. This work was perfect; I'd get out of the house a couple of days a week for meetings but would be around for the kids, slotting projects in mostly around their naptimes and the few hours their grannie offered to babysit. I grew slowly, making sure I wasn't on my computer too much when the kids were around but wanting to be ambitious enough to make a success out of this fledgling business. I wasn't rolling in cash by any means but I was starting to feel like this was something I could manage, and within nine months I'd paid my parents back the car loan. After almost three years of surviving on a small maternity allowance and feeling guilty every time I spent my husband's money, this was the biggest success I could have hoped for. Paying back that loan was the boost I needed; it gave me the confidence I'd been lacking when it came to believing in the future of myself as a bread-winner, a provider.

After a year of my consultancy an opportunity came up to interview at BBH, a worldwide ad agency, as a team manager for a six-month contract that I was assured would go permanent. I thought it over and decided it was too good a chance to pass up and was offered the job after my first interview. I knew my own marketing consultancy was something I wanted to develop in the future, so I thought this would be a wonderful chance to learn how the big boys did business.

My six months at BBH were a great experience and I worked with big companies like Mentos, Graco and Virgin Media. I felt like I'd got some semblance of myself back; I was the woman who was driven enough to get up at six in the morning to travel from Milton Keynes to London for work and, though the hours were gruelling, I loved the fact that I no longer worked on my tod in my lonely kitchen with only the radio for company, but in an actual office with actual people! I was the hands-on leader of the digital execution team and together we worked on some amazing products, including the launch of the new Gordon's Gin ad online over Christmas. It felt so empowering to know I'd started to have a career, an actual career, like I'd read about in the pages of *Glamour* magazine. It was something I'd never ever craved before but I got such a buzz from it now – I started to realise how much I wanted to make a success of myself not only as a mother but in business as well.

Working within such a large and fast-paced company had its disadvantages, though. I was the only member on my team with kids, and though as manager I was the leader of the pack I was also the one to leave on the dot of five thirty, sneak off at three for a harvest festival or skulk in an hour late because I'd been at a recorder concert. On more than one occasion my Milton Keynes MD – a man with a stay-at-home wife, natch – pointedly asked me to remind my team that ours was not a 9–5 job and that 'early' leavers were being noticed.

As we were all working in advertising there was a huge work hard/play hard ethos: presenteeism was a huge problem, with kudos (and promotions) being given to those who worked the hardest, i.e. spent the longest time at their desks (whether they were actually working or not seemed to be irrelevant; in fact, from what I could tell those who were lauded the most for their 'work-hard' attitudes were the ones who spent the long evenings in the office on Facebook). I'd always be on my laptop catching up on projects post-bedtime, but it didn't seem to count unless my bum was firmly on my office seat or my face was present in yet another time-wasting meeting with creative directors bickering over a font or the placement of a comma in some copy. Who cares? I would wonder. It made me so frustrated to be a part of this white noise when I could have been at home mothering my children instead.

The days of such meetings and stupid work-based politics felt, to me as a mum, exhausting. When I had a sick baby needing me at home or a toddler wanting me to help with her phonics, having to hang around the office while a business lead discussed in depth some irrelevant points of an advertising strategy with someone who wasn't even on the account made me want to shoot myself in the face. I came to realise how much unnecessary crap and noise goes on in workplaces, how much pandering to egos and how many unnecessary politics there are. I just wanted to get in, do my job and get out again: something that my colleagues seemed to feel was a foreign way of working.

I also missed out on the fun social aspects of working in such a fast-paced industry, despite having so much enjoyed this aspect of my career pre-kids. At BBH we had a bar in our office, *an actual bar in our office,* but come Friday afternoon I'd always be too knackered/shouldered with child-related responsibilities to take advantage of the free booze. I hated having to wave good-bye to my colleagues as they merrily necked Coronas or Sauvignon Blanc, instead shooting home for nursery pick-up time and the weekend supermarket run.

Speaking of which, the whole nursery thing almost made the time I spent at work not worth it. I was lucky to have my mother nearby – she looked after my children two days a week – but for the other three I was at the mercy of paid childcare and the logistics of it were mind boggling. I shuttled my children between two childcare settings, a village preschool and nursery, and boy, was it expensive (and confusing – once or twice I turned up to nursery when the kids should have been at preschool, or vice versa). I went back to full-time work as a single parent six months before Elfie went to school, and for that period of time I relied on a small amount of savings to supplement my income. It wasn't that my salary wasn't good – it was great – but childcare was just so damn expensive. With both kids needing to be looked after, some months I was shelling out £1,600 on nurseries: SIXTEEN HUNDRED POUNDS. That's enough to go on a not-bad all-inclusive holiday in Europe for a week, which would have been a lovely thing to do had I not been working so many hours.

(Ironically, thanks to nursery rules, on the couple of occasions we did go on an all-inclusive holiday in Europe for a week I still had to pay my nursery fees. It would have been more satisfying to literally burn the cash, if I'm honest.)

It wasn't all bad, though. Not working at home meant I had an excuse to wear lovely outfits every day, actually utilising the items in my wardrobe that were neither Breton tops, made of jersey nor covered in Ready Brek; and my London office was on Carnaby Street, right behind Liberty of London, i.e. the best shop ever to peruse in your lunch hour (if you have any spare cash left over after your extortionate nursery fees, that is). Plus being in London so often gave me time to indulge the new hobby I'd discovered: Tinder swiping! The calibre of gentleman I'd be shown on Tinder in the capital was totally different to that which I'd find in Milton Keynes, and though I had neither the time nor energy to ever actually meet anyone after work, the swiping was still good fun.

I enjoyed the status that came with working for such a huge behemoth of an advertising institution, so when I found out our team in Milton Keynes was to be relocated permanently to London I was pretty gutted. I'd signed up to commute a couple of times a week but, with my kids so young and my need to be present at so many assemblies/doctor's appointments/pick-up times, I just couldn't make the full-time London life work. Like many big companies that judge productivity on how present their staff are, BBH was not a fan of flexibility for parents working from home despite the London MD being a mother of two young children – a fact that frustrated me no end – and so I waved goodbye to my fancy advertising lifestyle.

Though I wasn't quite ready to go full pelt on my own consultancy I still felt pretty bruised by having to leave a job that, despite the hours, egos and politics, I had loved, and was hesitant to go head-first into another position. In the same way as I hadn't wanted to commit to a relationship in the years post-marriage, I also didn't want to commit to a job that I wasn't sure I'd be totally in love with, so a return to freelancing seemed to be the best option. Which was how I ended up interviewing for a position as an account director at a local hospitality-specific (restaurants, bars and food – more interesting than it sounds, trust me), marketing agency. It was just a ten-minute drive from home – brilliant! I'd be working with the boyfriend of an old work pal – fab! They embraced the flexible-working ethos – a dream! I accepted a three-day-a-week freelance position with them and hit the ground running, quickly scaling up to four days because they asked and because I'm an idiot who can't say no to authority.

For that same reason I quickly became a full-time head of marketing, meaning my cushy freelance job was all of a sudden a proper role with long hours and major accountability. I hated it and soon realised why many professionals before me had quickly vacated the role I'd taken up: the team was a nightmare and the boss even more so. I had accepted the position thinking the life I led of a single mum was accepted and considered, but I soon found myself being expected to attend 7.30 a.m. leadership meetings and 8 p.m. client events. I spent the entire time having to call in favours from friends and family for childcare, and feeling like I was letting my children down: I wasn't there for school drop-offs, I wasn't there for school pick-ups, I wasn't there on sick days and even when I was there I wasn't, so wedded to my email was I. To be honest, the best things about the job were the fact that I got to tell people I was a 'head of marketing' and the peace of mind that I'd get a big salary at the end of the month.

The job was really hard, having to work as I did with an inherited, fractured team and many an incomplete project left by my predecessor. My CEO rode me like a horse, praising the things I did well – which I thought were many in the circumstances – but coming down like a ton of bricks on the things that weren't as she'd do herself. And she was an alpha female with sky-high expectations who took absolutely no prisoners, so these occasions were many and harsh.

This job, coupled with the ongoing work with my freelance consultancy, left me working eighty hours a week and I was *exhausted*. For the first time in my life I didn't have to budget and could spend money like Monopoly notes (I shopped at Diane Von Furstenberg and Jimmy Choo for my work wardrobe, for Pete's sake: I felt like Milton Keynes' answer to Paris Hilton), but by God I was miserable. Spending hours chugging up and down the motorway in my Ford Focus (I'd saved up enough to buy a new one by then, and all on my own), I was bloody knackered.

One memorable day I'd travelled to see a client in Derbyshire before returning to the home counties for a lunch meeting and I was more tired than I've ever felt, so much so that I had no option other than to pull over at Northampton services, fifteen minutes from home, and take a nap right there in the car park.

My breaking point came one evening on my sofa at home, the children asleep upstairs: they went to bed with military precision back in those days, such was my need to have my life regimented so I could get the maximum amount of work squeezed into the minimum amount of time. I know, I know, I was a barrel of laughs back in the day (no wonder I was chronically single).

As I was banging away at my laptop in front of *Gilmore Girls* (was there anything better to watch than a single mother who was totally winning at life when you felt like you were failing yourself?) on a proposal that had a deadline of the next morning, an email pinged into my in-box – it was the dreaded boss, making yet another curt demand of me that, with my insane workload, I knew I would be unable to honour.

I burst into tears, thoroughly sick of the sight of my boss's name popping up when I really didn't want to see it. Though I was slowly morphing into an alpha female myself (a much kinder version than my CEO, I hasten to add), I still both revered and feared her, respecting her enormous success in business – from what I could tell built mainly on boozy lunches – and I desperately wanted her to like and respect me.

'I can't do this any more,' I sobbed into the keys of my laptop as Lorelai Gilmore flirted on-screen while sharing another cosy coffee with her daughter (is that what my relationship will be like with my daughter in the future?)

'I just can't. I hate this. I hate her. I don't want this,' I cried out loud.

I can't believe it had taken so long for the penny to drop, but finally, in that minute, it did.

'I *don't* have to do this any more,' I said, again out loud. My cries turned into manic laughs. 'I don't have to. I can just stop.'

The next day I walk into the office, carefully crafted resignation in hand, to tell that alpha female boss that I wasn't going to be the recipient of her tear-inducing emails any more. 'I'm sorry to hear that,' she tells me. I'm not, and I don't think she really is, either.

My notice period is two weeks and I feel like I'm flying as I walk out of the office that day. I'm free (or at least I will be at the end of my fourteen days), I'm no longer chained to what possibly might be the dullest clients in the whole of hospitality, I'm going to be able to take my kids to school in the morning and work from home, spending my lunch hour a mile away at the gym when I'm stressed or asleep when I've worked too late the night before, as I often do – it's a revelation, a wondrous revelation.

I still need to make money though, so it's back to drumming up freelance business. With a book launch campaign I recently managed having won an award, I feel confident and happy to talk myself up, and quickly snag a one-day-a-week contract working for a local business. Safe in the knowledge that I have enough money coming in to scrape by should I find myself without any other work, I relax into my job as work-at-home consult-ant, mum and blogger.

With my marriage firmly out the door, my blog becomes the most constant thing in my life. It's been a solid companion to me ever since that day when I found out I was pregnant and if I ever go a few days without writing in it I feel all weird and empty, neglectful of the happy and supportive community I've crafted around me. The blog has become an outlet, not just for my single-parenting woes and wins but for my musings on work, new relationships (or lack thereof) and my happily growing female friendships. Quite simply, I wouldn't be with-out it.

Working for myself gives me some interesting insights into the way my mind works. I realise just how much of my personality is interlinked with my job, and it's fascinating (if a little scary) to consider how much my habits and behaviours are influenced by my work's procedures and guidelines. I've always loved the word 'procrastination' – it's such a weird one, full of tongue-tripping sounds and syllables – but going full pelt and working for myself makes me realise what a world-class procrastinator I am myself. I spend hours working around my work without doing the actual job at hand, and it's exhausting. I miss having a boss breathing down my neck, a bitch one or not, ordering me around and holding me accountable.

I also realise that, similarly to many women in self-employment or gainfully working for others, I have an absolutely huge fear of failure that I just can't shake. My base level of monotonous and easy work that I could do while standing on my head asleep is good, but the thought of someone giving me a meaty, more difficult project that'll really get my synapses twitching? That terrifies me.

I find myself sidestepping interesting and exciting emails enquiring as to my work availability as it seems easier to ignore the things that will challenge and push me, and instead to stick with the boring day-to-day work that has me wanting to take those aforementioned lunchtime naps (if napping were a football team I'd be Barcelona: having two kids under two taught me to grab sleep when and wherever I can. I will never tire of my forty winks). I don't feel stretched by my everyday, simple projects but, even with three mouths to feed and a worrying Waitrose addiction, I find myself erring on the side of caution, missing out on the opportunities that could possibly really widen my horizons.

Every so often I'll have an attack of confidence and run through all those scary enquiry emails in my in-box, responding to them with one of the lame excuses we all use when we've been putting off responding to a message: 'You dropped straight into my junk mail!' is a favourite, or a simple 'I'm so sorry I missed your email coming in!' I imagine that, back in the pre-email days, it was a lot easier to swerve your responsibility to respond to communication you didn't want to engage with. I almost feel sad I'm not working in the early 90s and so have never been able to use the excuse of my fax machine running out of toner or my carrier pigeon getting lost.

It's this swerving of the scary emails that means I almost miss out on the chance to fulfil one of my biggest dreams: writing for a national newspaper. I've played at the art of scribing on my blog for five years now, and have come, I feel, pretty far in my writing: I'm mostly just blathering on my own website but as people are reading and responding I must be doing something right. But, lacking any professional writing-related qualifications (actually, lacking any professional qualifications at all, university dropout that I am), I've never considered what I do on my blog a job or career option, mainly because I enjoy it so much but also because well, it's just a blog, isn't it?

Claire Cohen, deputy women's editor of the *Telegraph*, doesn't think so. She writes to me to tell me she's just ignored her boyfriend for an entire weekend because she delved all the way back into my blog archives and loved every bit of them, and have I ever considered writing for a newspaper? 'ONLY EVERY SINGLE DAY, CLAIRE!' I want to respond with glee, 'only every single freaking day!'

But of course, I don't say that. I hop up and down a bit, tell my mum what AN ACTUAL EDITOR OF AN ACTUAL

BROADSHEET has said about my writing, and then promptly get too scared to reply to the email for an entire three weeks.

When I do pluck up the courage to respond ('Lovely to hear from you, so sorry I missed your email coming in!') I am even more delighted, yet terrified, at Claire's haste to book a meeting with me to discuss working together.

Shit the bed.

I'm so excited about taking an actual meeting with an actual editor that I turn up an entire twenty-four hours early, awkwardly sitting in the *Telegraph*'s cavernous atrium of a lobby for twenty minutes before Claire comes up to me to tell me that, although I am an idiot who is too overwhelmed to manage my diary properly, she will happily see me if I return at the appropriate time the next day (note: she doesn't say these things to me; I've taken a little artistic licence with what I imagine she was thinking at the time). I'm so awed by Claire's presence, her quiet confidence, sleek bob and outfit that is dead fashionable but not outlandishly so: I desperately want to be a part of this world, this glass-and-chrome office, this blow-dried hair and understatedly dressed persona.

I return the next day feeling slightly less flustered and sweaty and am thrilled to be offered the chance to write a column – A COLUMN – for the online version of the newspaper. I bite her metaphorical hand off at the chance to write for the mainstream media and rush home to start thinking of subject matter I can pitch to Claire.

My first column to go live is a thoughtfully penned 700 words on the subject of dating and sex as a single parent. What I had thought was a tongue-in-cheek and humorous take on the matter is received slightly differently, with some keyboard-warrior commenters taking severe umbrage at the fact that there's a woman with a libido let loose in a Conservative newspaper (oh my God! Alert the elders) and others inviting me out on dates (I go on one, of which more later).

Despite constant urging from Claire not to 'feed the trolls', I find it hard to keep a dignified silence when it comes to the comments section, particularly when I write a piece on the astronaut Tim Peake. Thinking of it as just another amusing take on motherhood – the humour perhaps being something that didn't translate so well to *Telegraph* readers – my article lambasts the respected astronaut and space explorer for buggering off to space for months and leaving his poor wife to deal with the in-laws over Christmas. Funny, right?

Apparently not.

The thing is, I have learned that when you write a story to appeal to the masses, as you must in a national newspaper, you have to come across as having a pretty solid and strong opinion on whatever it is you're writing about, whether that's Tim Peake or single-mum shagging. I maintain that outside of Katie Hopkins there aren't that many people who have such forthright (and mostly wrong) opinions, but if like me you're of the 'live and let live' school of thought you have to develop a pretty black-and-white way of writing about your opinions, even if you're not completely sure that's actually the way you feel about the subject at hand. Nobody wants to read your kind, respectful and waffly thoughts on single parents; they want to watch you slag off our home-grown heroes and then get taken down for it.

Plus, in the current world of oversaturated online media and a digital journalism industry that is 90 per cent based on clickbait, you may well end up having material published that you either don't totally agree with or plain old didn't write. I had fun on one occasion (and when I say fun I mean 'not fun at all') trying to explain to Will that, although I had written the article he'd seen published on one of the biggest websites in the country, I didn't write the title that screamed I'd been forced against my will to live with a man I was married to. Oh and, no, I wouldn't be able to get it changed. Sorry again, Will.

Having aspired to write for the mainstream media for as long as I can remember, I found these difficult lessons to learn. My mum gently enquired more than a few times if I thought I was selling my soul by penning all these brutally honest and strongly opined articles that weren't 100 per cent me, and though I really enjoyed the fact that my readership had gone from 2,000 daily to half a million via the (often awful) readers of the *Telegraph* online, I couldn't help but agree with her.

But still I kept at it, knowing that if I wanted to touch other women with the stories of what I'd been through in my journey to single parenthood, make an eventual success of my blog and perhaps even write a book one day (oh, hello there!) I'd have to have a large platform to launch off.

There were, however, pieces I was proud of in between my light-hearted bitching over Tim Peake, open letters to Angelina Jolie ('You don't need no man!!' etc etc) and musings over sex. After changing my name back soon after my ex-husband and I separated, I wrote about what this process, one of the most important decisions I felt I'd made since Will had left, had meant to me. I also wrote what I felt was an emotion-filled account of how it feels to be without your children at Christmas time (in a nutshell, it's fucking shit) and my single cockles were warmed to see how many people this piece resonated with, how many single parents contacted me with their own difficult experiences.

It felt good to be fulfilling one of my longest-held dreams, clickbaity titles and trolls included. More importantly, though, it was one of my jobs (albeit not a very well-paid one) that I could do from home while making sure the children had me around as much as they needed. And knowing I was completely and unequivocally at home for them whenever they needed me made me proudest of all.

CHAPTER ELEVEN

Back On The Market

Three weeks after my husband moves out I set up a profile on Match.com. I'm back 'on the market': a phrase that simultaneously makes me feel delighted, nervous and like a 1960s semi on RightMove. With the dating world (I mistakenly thought) at my feet, I decide this is my time; this is my opportunity to meet my Prince Charming, my Prince William even: the man of my dreams.

It feels early to be back 'out there', early to consider casting aside my ten-year relationship for a fling. But I have felt so void of attention, so craving of warmth and company, that all I want to do is sit opposite someone in a bar who gives me smiles and compliments, no matter who they are.

I initially approach my dating life in completely the wrong way, going out with the first man from Match.com who asks. Having been in a marriage for so long that was teetering on a precipice between success and failure (and leaning steeply in the direction of failure) I'm so thankful for his positive attention that I would have lapped it up whether it came from him or

Hitler: it didn't matter; I just wanted the dates and the kind company. Not that Pizza Express particularly counts as hot date action but hey, I'm a twenty-seven-year-old single mother who has spent the last year going quietly mad. I'll take my wining and dining where I can get it.

The first man I go out with is Andy, a vertically challenged ski instructor some fifteen years my senior, whose ex-wife left him when she found out about a torrid affair he was having with a woman in her early twenties. He lives in the dodgy area of town and doesn't use grammar in his text messages, yet in my deluded and heartbroken state I think he's perfect. He takes me out for the odd two-for-one mai tai and slings a Nando's in my general direction every once in a while and I'm hooked. For a couple of months, anyway.

I know it's not going to work when I, the enthusiastic home cook, go over to his house for a promised romantic night in, something that has set my expectations sky high. Going by what I've seen on the telly of cosy home dates I'm expecting candles, flowers, chilled wine and three courses. Instead I'm seated at the kitchen table with a beer, all offers of help rebuffed as he sets to cooking my meal, a meal that's looking to be just the one course but is at least being slaved over by someone else: a treat I haven't experienced in far too long.

I'm impressed that he's whipping me up a spaghetti Bolognese, knowing as I do that he has experience of teaching skiing in the Italian Alps. Does he have a secret recipe from his European experiences that he's going to employ to really impress me this evening?

No. He really, really doesn't.

This evening's dinner is courtesy of the Costco frozen aisle.

I'm not joking when I say that every single aspect of the meal, apart from the dried pasta and tinned tomatoes, is cooked from frozen. And, outside my brief sojourn in student halls, I've never seen anything like it.

The frozen onions go in first with a bit of vegetable oil, followed by some frozen carrots and mushrooms. They get a bit of a stir while another bottle of beer is drunk and tins are cranked open. Two tins of tomatoes are sloshed in and cooked ('simmered' is too much of a technical word for what is going on in front of me) before the final stage of the process: the beef. In my kitchen I usually cook the beef first, painstakingly browning it off on a low heat and then adding the other ingredients and cooking until the meat takes on the flavours of the best beef stock, red wine and fresh oregano. I've never cooked with beef that is prepared quicker than pasta before and, though I'm disgustingly fascinated in a can't-look-away, car-crash kind of way, I'm also kind of impressed.

Dinner is served with a flourish alongside dried Parmesan from the cupboard and I am presented with a full plate. It's better than I expected: it's not haute cuisine but it's not school-dinner levels of terrible, either. I'm fascinated, not by his cooking skills but by how not-terrible it is. It could have, should have, been a lot worse.

The next week I invite him round to my house to return the favour, deciding to cook a rack of crusted lamb with minted peas, dauphinoise potatoes and a lamb *jus* alongside a lovely Bordeaux that I've chosen specially. I present the most gorgeous plate of food, proud as Punch to have spent hours slaving over a beautiful meal that afternoon with the children buzzing around my ankles. He looks at it, his face not conveying the impression of awe and excitement that in my opinion he should be feeling (did I mention? I'm a total food snob. Yep).

'This meat isn't cooked,' he says.

'It's a rack of spring lamb,' I explain. 'It's supposed to be pink.'

'I can't eat it,' he tells me. 'Can you cook it a bit more? And have you got any beer?'

So I return to the hob while my own beautifully prepared rack of lamb gets cold on the table, cooking his meat off until it's a completely unappetising shade of brown and most likely the texture of old boots. I redeliver his food to him along with his beer – he can have it straight from the can at this point – and finally tuck in. My own lamb is beautiful, cold but beautiful.

After two months of seeing Andy a couple of times a week, and realising quite firmly that he's not the one for me or indeed, one who I want to spend any amount of time with, I tell myself I have to break up with him. But I haven't broken up with anyone since I was eighteen, when I told my soon-to-be ex-boyfriend that I didn't want to go out with him any more because I fancied his housemate instead (his housemate was a member of the Klaxons, do you blame me?). The boyfriend I had after that one was Will, and we all know how that story ends.

I ponder this for a few days, hoping I will find an answer to my situation that doesn't involve me saying the words out loud: 'I don't want to see you any more.'

Luckily I don't have to.

It is the Easter holidays and I've agreed to look after Andy's children for the afternoon while he works. His boys are older than my kids – six and nine – but are pleasant enough. Plus, even though I know by now that I don't want to be with him, I still have this inexplicable urge to impress him.

And so I take the kids, all of them, his and mine, to soft play for the afternoon. We follow that with McDonald's and then return to Andy's house to entertain ourselves until he gets back.

The afternoon wears on and they, as kids of a certain age do, start whining about getting the iPads out, so I let them. One of his sons takes an interest in my own iPad over his dad's, the range of games being a lot more interesting or something, so I let him play while I take charge of the other device. And thank goodness I do, because as I sit in their father's house looking after his children, he's 'at work' busily texting the so-called ex-girlfriend his wife left him over.

As his iPad account is linked to his mobile phone I am able to watch the iMessages roll in and go out as they happen. It's like a textual soap opera. It feels incredibly voyeuristic, almost rude to be watching such an intimate exchange, but I'm glued.

'Do you love her though?' she asks of him, obviously talking about me.

'Of course I don't,' says he. 'I will only ever love you.'

'But you're always spending time with her,' she says.

'Every time I'm with her I think of you,' is his response.

My first reaction to their exchange is shock. Though my marriage to Will was bad at its end, we were ultimately always respectful to one another, would never do anything to wound the other.

My husband had never – to my knowledge, anyway – been unfaithful or deceitful, and certainly never unkind, so I feel unprepared for this sort of situation. How on earth am I supposed to react or respond? Should I get upset? Probably.

I didn't, though. I mean, I let him know that nobody should ever be treated that way; nobody should be made to feel like they're the only one while another woman is being told they love her, so I made very sure that he felt ashamed of himself for that, confronting him with the messages (I took pictures of them so he couldn't weasel out of it). But I didn't actually care about it – not really.

I was ultimately quite relieved to have an excuse to finish the relationship without having to actually finish the relationship. The situation was a godsend, in fact. My days of overcooking lamb were over.

There's a spot on the floor in my bedroom where I like to cry. It's right next to my bed, where my cosy IKEA sheepskin rug sits. I weep in various positions on this spot, sometimes curled up in the foetal position as I sob into my hands, often on my knees leaning on the bed as I fold my arms in front of me and cry that way.

Most of the time there's music in the background, something innocuously soothing like Bon Iver or Damien Rice, both soundtracks to my misery that I can no longer listen to outside of this context because of the emotions they evoke – happier memories of my marriage, of being on holiday, dancing at my wedding and endless evenings spent with my ex-husband.

The crying always lasts a while and, without exception, happens while the children are asleep: the last thing I want to do is pass my discontent on to them or cause any upset in their little innocent lives. I'm quiet with the crying because I don't want to wake them and, as I now live in a terraced house, I don't want to worry my neighbour. Jenny is in her late sixties and on her own too; she got divorced twenty years ago and I know she'll have an eye out for these kinds of emotional outbursts, but I'd rather our conversation revolved around the children or the health of Florence, her elderly cat, than the sound of my sad sobbing penetrating her walls.

I am lonely, so very lonely. Perhaps not quite as lonely as I felt in my marriage, but now instead of just being lonely I'm both lonely and alone, which feels worse somehow, much more tragic.

I'm grieving the loss of my husband terribly. It's a difficult thing, to come to terms with the fact that the life I thought I had ahead of me is no more, and I'm not quite sure what to do with these feelings. It's like I am still in love with my husband, but not the person he is today, not the person I said goodbye to some twelve months previously: I'm still in love with the man he was ten years ago, the man he was when we first met, and I'm finding it really difficult to reconcile this version of him with who he is today. I wonder if I've also changed beyond recognition in this time, wonder if he looks back on our relationship and feels the same tugs of nostalgia and sadness that I do.

I desperately want him back. I crave the man I chose to be my husband and the father of my children, not the distant version who picks up his kids from me once a fortnight with a cursory hello. But this man, the one I loved, he's gone – he's not there any more. He acts like he's the same but he isn't; he doesn't see how he's changed, and I miss who I have come to think of as 'the old Will' an incredible amount.

I find it very hard to watch how he's moved on when I feel like I'm stuck standing still, even though I've gone through the motions of dates and new jobs. I might have found my feet in a career I'm starting to love but I'm struggling on so many other fronts: feeling secure where I live, feeling secure in my finances, feeling secure about having so much responsibility when it comes to the children and, most importantly, feeling secure in myself. I don't know who I am without a husband and, though I don't show it, day-to-day I am extremely wobbly alone.

In a kind of desperation at this situation I decide the easiest thing to do is to get partnered up again, to have the solidity of a husband by my side. And so I look to the path of least resistance: my ex-husband. Who, as we haven't actually pushed ahead with a divorce yet, is technically still my husband. We've only been apart for six months so I'm sure he'll be open to talk of reconciliation, of reuniting with his family, who, I reason, he must miss terribly, so I invite him in for a chat one evening as he's dropping the kids off.

I sit him down and explain that hey, people make mistakes, and are you sure we're doing the right thing? I tell him we've got these beautiful kids between us as well as almost ten years of shared history, and we should really give our marriage another go before we decide to fuck up our family for ever.

Will looks at me like I've grown an extra head. In fact I think he would rather I had grown an extra head than asked him if we could get back together; that would have been a situation he would have known better how to deal with.

'No,' he says incredulously, quite rightly almost chuckling at the madness of what I'm saying. 'There's no way we can get back together.'

And so, once more, I cry.

'I can't do this alone,' I sob. 'I never wanted to do this alone. Come home, we'll do couples counselling, we'll do anything – just come and be a father to your children.'

For the second time, he leaves.

Of course, my asking my soon-to-be ex-husband to come home to me is literally one of the most irrational things I've ever done (and, as a woman with severe post-natal depression, I have done a few irrational things in my time). We are better apart and weren't supposed to be a couple – if I've learned anything in the last six months, it's that – but the loneliness has well and truly got me pinned. It's not even the practical bits and pieces that have me on my knees any more but, more embarrassingly, the emotional stuff. I've now learned where to find my gas meter (next to the front door, duh) and was bought a toolkit when I moved into my first house alone (thanks, Dad!), but a multi-bit ratchet screwdriver and a meter-box key do not a husband replacement make. They don't spoon you when you're lonely and scared at night, for one.

I hear this loneliness experience of mine a lot in the divorce journeys of friends, too: no matter how unhappy our marriages were, how dysfunctional the relationships, we'd become completely conditioned to a life with another person, our since departed partners. Despite knowing our specific coupledoms weren't working for us, removing ourselves from these partnered situations left us lost, lonely and sad. We find it hard to strike out and find a way on our own as we've been so used to operating as part of a couple, or a family.

After too many nights spent crying on the floor of my bedroom I realise I need to do something about this misery. Enough feeling sorry for myself, enough mooning about after my marriage that was (but now isn't) – just, basically, enough. I need to pick myself up and find something that'll make me happy. And, with my first weird dating experience with Andy done and dusted, a boyfriend is a good place to start.

Lacking any better ideas, I decide to approach my dating life from an entirely formulaic and methodical angle. I assess the situation as I would a particularly tricky work project, wanting to divide and conquer, taking names and kicking arse. I resolve that it'll be a numbers game, and that it's up to me to sift through the wheat to find the chaff.

As I had met my ex-husband at eighteen I had precisely zero experience of dating pre-marriage so, when I became single, I was quite keen to get 'out there' and discover this new exciting world of men and dates. Having grown up with *Sex and the City* as my best reference for the experiences of single gals, I believed that my life was about to change: my wardrobe would suddenly develop a collection of Manolo Blahnik shoes and I'd spend my weekends quaffing cosmopolitans with eligible bachelors.

But Manhattan proved to be somewhat different from Milton Keynes and the realities of dating as a mum soon become clear: how on earth was I supposed to fit my children, a career, sleep and a fledgling sex life into my limited time alone?

With great difficulty, it would seem.

As a married person I always enjoyed meeting new people and discovering new things, so I reckoned my dating life should be no different. I expected glittering conversation over bottles of wine, interesting individuals who would change my perspective on life and love, and I figured that as an approaching-thirty mum of two with only two evenings off a fortnight my spare time was precious: I didn't want to spend time with men who didn't fit my idea of perfection – or, at least, who didn't get close to it.

One of the best things about online dating is that you can assess your potential dates for the qualities you're hunting down before you even go out with them. The online profile is a great start: is it well spelled? Is grammar used correctly? Are they funny yet informative? Do they show their teeth when they smile (a closed-lip smile usually means bad teeth)? Are there any selfies featuring a messy bedroom or a urinal? Do they live within a twenty-mile radius of you? Once you'd ticked off all the points on your 'must-haves' list via their profile it was OK to introduce yourself to them via message, at which point you'd get more of a feel for who they were.

One of the worst things about online dating is that the emailing portion of the game allows you to create some kind of false impression of intimacy with someone you've never met before. When looking for a potential partner you want to find out everything you possibly can about their life in the little text box provided by Guardian Soulmates, but boy does that usually backfire when you meet up with them in real life a couple of weeks later. The thing is, when your heart and mind are open to meeting new people, you become eager to connect to them pre-date, even if they're a person you wouldn't look twice at in a crowded bar – which, confusingly, you don't know until you meet them in real life. I lost count of how many blokes I got on well with via the medium of online dating platforms – when they had time to think and formulate interesting responses to my probing questions – but whom I was disappointed by when it came to meeting up face-to-face and speaking in actual real life. It was quite tedious and always frustrating.

It was almost easier to use dating apps like Tinder, where the expectations were slightly lower and less time input was required. I quite liked the cut-throat feeling of swiping yes or no, making snap decisions on men because I didn't like the cut of the over-head lighting in their bedroom profile photo (very important for future happiness, I reckon). I swiftly developed a system for weeding out the good ones: no kids in photos, (how could my future dreamboat not be as concerned about lurking Tinder paedophiles as I was?) no smeared and dirty mirrors, no flexed muscles and, as above, no bloody urinals.

So focused was I in my quest for the perfect man that I decided to draw up a list of things I wanted in one. My thought was that, if they didn't tick off at least half of the things on my list, then they probably weren't going to be the one for me. I mean, if methodical, precise and ambitious worked for me at work, why wouldn't it apply to my love life, too?

Thinking hard, I drew up eighteen points:

- Intelligent, or at least well-educated.
- Tall, preferably taller than 6 foot.
- Older than me, probably between the ages of thirty-two and forty.
- Doesn't live at home with his parents.

- Lives near me.
- Likes music, but not bad music.
- Has a challenging career that he loves and is passionate about.
- Likes fancy food and to be cooked for. And cheeseburgers.
- Respects and encourages my career.
- Likes children, maybe has some – but doesn't advertise them to the weirdos stalking their profile.
- Has a great sense of humour (by which I mean 'laughs at my jokes').
- Hot (duh).
- Plays some sort of sport or at least goes to the gym.
- Is fairly cultured, or at least likes to pretend to be.
- Looks good in a suit.
- Looks good out of a suit.
- Understands the value of a nice pair of shoes.
- Believes in chivalry.

And so I set about my dating game. I went out with investment bankers, entrepreneurs, CEOs, twenty-five-year-olds (I KNOW), journalists, comedians, marketing executives, academics . . . you name them, I've dated them (probably). I sat through endless hours of strangers regaling me with stories of their 'colourful' lives (I'll be the judge of that, pal). I drank red wine in at least four different counties and in front of sixteen different open fires, and the only reason I didn't start a blog about all these awful dates was because my mum told me it would have been mean to.

It's amazing how sterile and calculated the process started to feel. I'd meet someone and immediately assess them for the points I was looking for. If they didn't fit? Game over.

In the course of my dating I met many thirty- and forty-some-things who were just desperate to settle down with a woman who'd happily cook for them and massage their egos for the rest of their lives and, I have to tell you, as lonely as I was I just wasn't quite down for that. To be honest, I had my own ego to take care of and there really wasn't going to be time to look after anyone else's. I started to understand my single girlfriends' wails when they'd come to me complaining about how they couldn't find a boyfriend. Granted, the dates seemed to be easy to come by, it was just the quality of them that was a bit dubious.

Really, I just wanted to meet someone with whom I'd share a bit of chemistry and perhaps some interests and hobbies. When I first became single I hadn't thought that was a huge ask but, as I got deeper into my experiences of dating, I started to feel more and more envious of the eighteen-year-old me who'd met her perfect match in the most innocent of ways. I understood that I was an adult now, a mother, and had different thresholds and expectations when it came to the opposite sex, but why was this finding-a-man thing so freaking hard? I was a good person: where was my Prince Charming, Mark II?

CHAPTER TWELVE

Mr Right (Or Mr Right, No Way)

As rough as the dating experience is, as much of a waste of time as I often believe it to be, I never get bored of going on a first date. I approach them keeping a motto my mum always used to say to me in the back of my mind: 'They probably won't be the love of your life, but their best friend might be.' And to be honest, as a work-from-home single mum I welcome the company of any adult, even if my date is slightly awkward or boring. I could have a good time conversing with a wall as long as I was wearing a nice outfit and had a glass of Sauvignon Blanc in my hand.

In my experiences of dating I soon come to realise that the phrase 'There's nowt so queer as folk' must have been coined by a woman who'd been using Tinder too long. I have friends who call me monthly purely to hear my latest updates on the latest oddballs I've gone for drinks with and boy, do I always deliver.

Not only is dating quite a foreign concept to me, but doing it with two kids in tow brings a whole other level of trickiness, and as with so many other parts of my life as a single mum this is both logistical and emotional. The men who swipe right on me, a twenty-seven-year-old woman, do not expect me to come laden with baggage, and though Elfie and Hux are the most important people in *my* life I am quite aware that for some men they might be two children too many. Though deep down I know my mum is once again correct when she tells me that my Prince Charming will be a man who embraces children and the huge list of positives that comes with them, I still find myself hiding the fact that they exist like a pint-sized dirty mistress.

They don't appear on my dating profiles – I don't want to advertise their existence to people I've never met before – and I usually wait until I win a potential date over with my wit and charm before I announce them. Revealing the fact that I have kids goes down like a cup of cold sick with some blokes, while others remain unfazed, and I am never able to gauge which way it's going to go. It's something I lose sleep over and, I hate the fact that I get so nervous wondering whether men I don't know if I like will negatively judge me for the two most precious people I have, my two biggest achievements. By my reckoning, they should feel bloody lucky to be given the chance to have Elfie and Hux in their lives.

Before long I start to get annoyed with myself that I'm letting this worry me so much, and in a fit of defiance I decide to go on a date without revealing my kids' existence to my prospective beau. The man in question is David, a dashing thirty-seven-year-old security specialist working for a bank in the City with a double degree from Cambridge: 'Score!' I think. David has all the benefits of working in finance – an interesting job, a high level of intelligence, personal solvency – without the arrogance of a banker. Plus he describes himself as a fan of pogonotrophy in his online dating profile, the first time a man has caused me to google a word – one that sounds quite similar to pornography but is thankfully very different – in this situation (Pogonotrophy: The act of cultivating, or growing and grooming, a moustache, beard, sideburns or other facial hair. So now you know).

I like the irreverence of his profile, so we arrange our date, without me telling the bearded one that I've got two children snuggled up in their beds at home.

The beginning of the night goes swimmingly: I feel confident and happy in the outfit I've chosen and the venue, a local wine bar, is pleasingly buzzing. The man sitting across from me, though probably a bit shorter than stipulated on my 'ideal man list', is nice enough, and I'm happy to be out of the house and in the land of the 3D people on a Friday night.

After an hour of pleasant conversation, I decide that I like and trust this man enough to want to divulge to him my parental status.

'I have something I should probably tell you,' I say.

He leans in with a cocked eyebrow, 'Oh yes? Do tell . . .'

I take a deep breath. My hands are sweating and I'm shaking a little. I worry about his reaction: will he storm out? Call me a liar? Say something awful about unmarried women with kids? I'm scared and I take a gulp of my cocktail – a porn-star martini, all class – before I go on.

'I've got two children,' I bumble. 'They're one and three. I'm sorry I didn't tell you before, I didn't know whether I should or not—'

He cuts me off with a laugh. 'I know you have two children,' he says. 'I looked you up.'

I am stunned. 'But I didn't give you my surname,' I say, thinking that he must have to hand some kind of IT specialist genius database that enables him to match the first names and photographs of his dates with their full family and work histories. I ask him as much.

'Nah,' he says with a smile, 'I just googled "Alice Milton Keynes".'

Opening a browser on my iPhone as he sits in front of me, I try typing in the same words myself and up pop the results: here's my blog, my Instagram, my Twitter account. There's no hiding on the internet, eh?

We have a laugh about it but when I get home I feel very exposed. I'm not comfortable that people are able to look me up so easily and I feel weird that David has been able to go online and read so much about me before we've even met. He knows details about my wedding, my children's births, my divorce, my post-natal depression. I think I would have felt less bare if I was naked on that date, sipping a porn-star martini in my birthday suit.

Luckily David is very kind and understanding about my blog, something that was back then a hobby rather than a career. Our relationship fizzles out after a few weeks but I remain thankful for his open mind when he could have used the information he had such easy access to in a completely different way.

That wasn't the only time my online presence has affected my love life.

Writing for the *Telegraph*, I had all sorts of weird and wonderful reader emails. Often these came from other lonely divorcees – many of whom were in the Middle East, funnily enough – and of course there were the odd few who prompted me to click the 'delete' button immediately (I had one anonymous correspondent who only ever signed off his emails 'Secret Admirer').

One email stood out to me. It was sent from a work email address – a City finance firm – from a guy called Tim who told me he was surfing the *Telegraph*'s women's section on a bored bank holiday. He introduced himself, complimenting my writing (always a sure-fire way to a writer's heart) and chatting generally about the kind of person he was. It was the perfect introductory email: light-hearted, informative, humorous and, crucially, not weird.

We met up for a date the next week in a bar in Covent Garden, sharing a bottle of red wine (I let him choose and was impressed that he went for a nice Malbec – append 'and wine snob' on to 'food snob' when you're next talking about me). Though we were both visibly nervous – outside of the olden-days lonely hearts columns, how often do people go on dates with prospective lovers they meet via the newspaper? – but conversation flowed and we had a laugh. Tim had a persistent cough and, around half an hour into the date, he asked if I smoked (the answer was a resounding 'No') before excusing himself to go outside for a cigarette. We talked about the habit of smoking when he returned to the table.

'It's not that I think it's *completely* despicable,' I explained. 'If you want to smoke, that's your choice to make. But the smell, the health implications, I just wouldn't want to be with a smoker. I hope you understand.'

'No need to worry about it,' he says, breathing second-hand nicotine over me. 'I used to smoke but I've given up!'

What followed was a short relationship that involved him spending most of the time sneaking off for a cigarette and then trying to pretend that he hadn't. Despite that, he was fun to hang out with, and I was happy to see him every so often, as long as it wasn't in his full-of-fag-fug house.

Our relationship came to a head one evening the week before Christmas at 10 Greek Street in Soho, one of my favourite restaurants. We'd sat down at a cosy table to enjoy some great food and delicious wine, and I tried to steer the conversation away from politics: as he was a staunch Tory, our outlooks wildly differed, something I found acceptable in a relationship situation (although the way he belittled my own more liberal and socialist views not so much).

From politics – and between breaks for him to step outside in the cold December air to puff on cancer sticks – the conversation swiftly moved to feminism and gender equality, a subject that, as a single mum and sensible human being, I hold close to my heart. In my new-found career and after my marriage, when I'd experienced life as a stay-at-home mum, I'd discovered a passion for equality (duh – why wouldn't you?) and was always keen to defend feminism wherever possible.

'Ah,' Tim said. 'You're a bra burner!'

I coughed and spluttered on a mouthful of wine. 'I wouldn't describe myself as a bra burner,' I told him. 'Feminism is the opportunity for women to choose a path that suits them in a way that doesn't discriminate – there's nothing radical or bra-burny about the movement.'

He raised his eyebrows and scoffed. 'You're all the same,' he said. 'Feminism doesn't actually exist – and it shouldn't. Can you imagine if women ruled the world? AWFUL! There's a reason why men are stronger, richer, more intelligent.' I couldn't believe my ears.

'What are you saying?' I asked. 'Don't you believe in gender equality, in closing the pay gap? Don't you think women are just as valid as men?'

'Course I don't!' he said. 'I want a wife who'll stay at home and raise my kids – who'll look after me. I expect I'll have to shell out for private schools, a gym membership and a 4x4, but that's a small price to pay. Women were put on the planet to look after their men. It's nonsense to believe anything else.'

In what was definitely not my proudest moment I stood up and threw a couple of banknotes on the table. 'I hope you find what you're looking for,' I said as I stormed out of the restaurant in a move that I may or may not have copied from a soap opera. Whatever; it felt good. I couldn't believe I'd spent so many weeks of my life dating a man who genuinely believed that men were better, somehow more valid, than women. How did I not know that he thought I was a lesser being than he? That I didn't deserve the same opportunities that he was offered? I felt like I needed to get home and take a shower, scrub myself clean of such dirty opinions.

Dating has this way, though, of bringing the weasels out of the woodwork. I've come across so many misogynists, oddballs and downright weirdos in my time on dating sites that it becomes quite laughable, my love life the punchline.

I'm amazed – and slightly downhearted – at how many men for example, actively date or spend time on dating apps when they are already in a supposedly committed and monogamous relationship. The number of men on Tinder in their wedding garb is genuinely surprising (and, in my opinion, completely tacky), and when you also factor in the men who are on websites and apps *pretending* to be single, the number becomes quite breathtaking.

I had a little experience of this, starting with one of the very first men I dated after my marriage split. Mike seemed too good to be true (which, it turned out, he was): an investment banker, a wine afficionado, an interesting accent and an interest in theatre . . . 'This dating lark's easy!' I thought.

Mike wined and dined me, firstly in Soho and then on a surprise date to watch *To Kill A Mockingbird* at Regent's Park Open Air Theatre. It was exactly what I had been waiting for in my pursuit of love; nice food, nice wine, a bit of culture. Perfect.

After three dates I went back to Mike's apartment, a small flat in Mayfair, packed to the rafters with wine coolers and photographs of his smiling children, who he clearly adored. His ex-wife lived in Kent with the children, he told me, and he returned to the family home every Friday or Saturday, staying until Monday when he'd return to work his long hours in the City. He coached his son's football team, spent his Saturday nights in bed with his young daughter snuggling. I thought it was lovely that, though divorced, he was still so devoted to his kids.

The relationship soon fizzled out as it was difficult to see each other when he was so often back and forth from his family home, which was a shame I thought; but my friends did not.

'Are you KIDDING?!' guffawed Kate in New York, when one evening I explained the situation over Skype to her. 'He's clearly still married.'

I was taken aback. 'But we had S-E-X,' I spelled out to her. 'Why would he do that if he was married?'

'Because he's a man, darling,' she explained. 'It's what the bastards do!'

And they did.

My next brush with a married man again came as a surprise, by which I mean he told me he was very much divorced. I met John on a dating website and he joined me for drinks in Soho after a work event on, ironically, International Women's Day. We drank dirty martinis at Dean Street Townhouse until my legs (and my lips) were wobbly and, I have to say, it was good fun.

John was twenty years older than me and the CEO of a big media company, and as he was so often out of the country it was difficult to get together for dinner or drinks. We dated sporadically, every eight weeks or so, but it was always interesting.

On our second date I got the distinct feeling that he was going to be one of those men who persevered in his pursuit of me until he got his end away and then swiftly buggered off, so even though I quite wanted to sleep with him (he was attractive: I'm only human) I didn't. My morals were evidently stronger than my libido. And so I continued to date him, enjoying the company but, wary of his intentions and not wanting to feel used, keeping him at arm's length.

It's worth saying that when you're doing any kind of dating, but particularly meeting people online, it's important to be safe and feel comfortable that the person you're meeting is who they say they are. Much like the research that IT security expert David did on me, as soon as I had a potential date's phone number I'd begin my routine of due diligence, working through a positively anal checklist of processes to make sure I knew exactly who they were. And, unless they've got their Facebook privacy settings on high (or – shock horror – aren't on social media), you can use this information to find out a veritable encyclopaedia of personal knowledge about people.

Media mogul John had checked out in all my initial investigations and, although he didn't have a social media presence, there was a wealth of trade press on him that confirmed his identity and job. So far, so good: I continued to date him feeling comfortable in the knowledge I wasn't being catfished, and even agreed on a Christmas date with him – yes, on 25 December – my children would be with their dad and I thought it'd be fun to do something out of the ordinary to save me feeling sad over the fact they wouldn't be around. A fun date with John would do the job nicely.

We met at one of my favourite bars in King's Cross; he had dropped his daughter off with his ex-wife in Buckinghamshire and I had travelled down from a family Christmas lunch at my auntie's house in Leamington Spa. It was our sixth date and I'd brought an overnight bag; with a host of cocktails in the offing and the trains not running until 27 December, the subtext was clear. Tonight would be the night to consummate.

The evening was fun. I swilled old-fashioneds and he drank mojitos as we sat at the bar and chattered about nothing in particular before going back to his house, a penthouse flat overlooking the *Mary Poppins*-esque rooftops of London. It was a world away from the first bloke's home I had visited, with nary a brown sheet or dodgy single bed in sight, only miles of chrome, marble and London views as far as the eye could see.

'I could get used to this,' I thought.

We did what I expected we would do and had a go at the horizontal mambo – it was OK, not earth-shattering, but OK (though in those days it was pretty much never earth-shattering) – and I stayed for breakfast the next morning. Over salmon, eggs and avocado, we synchronised diaries, booking in a dinner date in two weeks' time when he would be back from a New Year's Eve trip to Malaysia with friends – at least this is who he told me he was going away with. I looked forward to it.

I woke up one chilly January morning a couple of days before that dinner date: it was 6 a.m., the usual rising time for my daughter, and as always I felt around for my phone to give Instagram a cursory scroll before I got up for the day. I was pleasantly surprised to see two WhatsApp messages from John awaiting me, both sent a couple of hours previously.

'I don't think we should see each other any more,' the first one said.

'It's best if we leave it here and break contact immediately,' read the second.

Naive woman that I am, I immediately worried for him and shot over a message in reply: 'Is everything OK? What's happened?'

On WhatsApp, the daters' preferred method of communication, you can see when your messages have been both delivered to and read by the recipient, with two little ticks that turn blue when the text is read. This tool is sometimes paranoia-inducing but more often handy: it's a vital part of reading subtext in a relationship, especially when embarking on dates with blokes you don't know well. Does he read your messages and respond

171

immediately? He likes you. Responds only four hours after read-ing? Meh, don't get your hopes up.

On this January morning I saw there was only one tick on the return messages I'd sent to John, and one tick never turned into two: that meant he'd blocked me.

I was disappointed. Not because I particularly liked John or saw a future with him, but we'd had a nice time together and I didn't see why it had to end. I especially didn't see why it had to conclude in such an impersonal and brutal way: surely our six dates and subsequent night together warranted something of an explanation? Apparently not. What a dirty dog, I thought.

One of the reasons why I found motherhood so hard was because nobody feeds back to you about your performance. There's no three-monthly reviews, no one-to-one, no appraisals, no pay rises: it's really difficult to judge how well you're doing in your new role of mother with nobody to tell you outright, and I'm the kind of person who finds that very confusing and demo-tivating. And it's the same in relationships – I need the reassur-ance of someone to tell me what I am doing well, or not. And in the case of a relationship ending, well, if you don't want me to lie awake at night wondering what on earth I could have done that was so heinous, you need to tell me what's up.

So to have a relationship (and in this case, not even a relation-ship: a dalliance) end in such a way was very upsetting. I wanted a reason why I wasn't worth seeing again: was I too talkative? Too optimistic? Too much of a single mother? Not enough of a floozy? Terrible in bed?

I wanted answers but the one man who could give them to me had blocked me on all forms of contact. Incredibly mature

172

behaviour from a middle-aged man, I think you'll agree. I dwelled on the situation for much longer than I should have, worrying about how his behaviour reflected on me. To seek comfort I returned to my old friend Google, trying to discover answers in the search engine, the technology that rarely let me down. And this time I was on a mission.

In my previous searches I'd found John on Companies House, where I could see that he held an impressive sixty-five director-ships. I'd got bored of scrolling through them all and had stopped at around thirty-two, not realising there were others that listed his home address instead of his London-based business one. Just call me Nancy Drew: I had a lead. Mentally noting the name of the village he lived in, I appended that to his name and surname in the Google text box. Bingo! The first result produced an article on the house he had recently renovated. *With his wife*. The so-called ex-wife he had apparently recently divorced, the one he couldn't stand the sight of. The one who, if the looks of the shiny interiors of his palatial country pad were anything to go by, had also decorated his central London penthouse.

OK, so I was still blocked on his WhatsApp and I didn't fancy making the effort to call him from a different number to chal-lenge him on his marital status; nor did I want to make any grand statements by contacting The Wife and potentially making life difficult for her or their children. But I have to admit I was somewhat appeased by the thought that, in the great mystery of 'What Did I Do Wrong to Cause This Man to Not Want To See Me Again?', one of the overriding factors was that he was a monumental philandering douchebag.

I made sure that, moving forward in my dating life, I was even more thorough in my research on the men who wanted to date me. As soon as I'd been given their phone number I'd copy and paste it into the Facebook search bar, and nine times out of ten this would give me their profile and therefore their full name – bingo! It'd be 50/50 as to whether or not their profile was locked down; sometimes I could scroll through months of 'lads on tour' photographs and 'happy birthday Grandma' posts, but sometimes there'd be nothing to see here. No matter – the name was the most important thing and this is what you could use for your next stage of investigations.

Hopefully their first or surname would be a little bit unusual (Alice Judge-Talbot is pretty easy to Google, for example), but if not you take the name of the town the bloke lives in or whoever he works for (which is hopefully discoverable from his Facebook profile), add it to their name and stick it into the search engine. You'll probably have to comb through a couple of erroneous results, but this is a pretty sure-fire way to verify a man's identity. From here you can take a look at their work history on LinkedIn – you'll want to log out first or purchase a premium account so they don't catch you snooping on them – and see what they're up to on both Instagram and Twitter. Bob's your uncle! You can now rest safe in the knowledge that you're about to date an entirely normal and non-threatening man. Hooray.

This method of investigation has proved very useful to me over the years, even once saving me from a date with an actual sex offender. When we met at the bar of a pub in Camden on the occasion of my friend's birthday, he didn't seem predatory at

first. We chatted a little and I gave him my number before returning to my friends, saying he could drop me a text some time,
which he did the next week. Having been lulled into a false sense
of security as I'd already met him in real life (and therefore not
having carried out my usual due diligence), I agreed to go on a
date with him after a couple of hours chatting back and forth.
He suggested the Charlotte Street Hotel and I was impressed – I
couldn't wait.

The morning of the date I was pottering around the house,
working and doing the washing, and a text message came in
from him. I was at my computer as it dropped and I suddenly
realised I hadn't looked this guy up, so I began my rigmarole of
investigations.

And thank goodness I did.

I almost gave up when I couldn't find him on Facebook, but
he'd emailed me from work so I knew his surname (thankfully it
was fairly unusual) and the location of his house. As soon as I
typed in his full name and the area of London he lived in, an
article popped up from the local newspaper: three years previously my prospective beau had been caught trying to solicit sex
from underage girls online. He'd been arrested, given a suspended
sentence, made to sign the sex offenders' register and wasn't
allowed on social media – which was why I couldn't find him on
Facebook.

I felt sick. Not just because I'd almost sat across from a sex
offender while quaffing cocktails in one of my favourite bars in
London, but because of what this might have meant had I not
been so persistent and thorough in researching him. I'd
mentioned my children to him and he knew I was a single mum;

175

it wasn't worth thinking about what the motivations were behind him wanting to wine and dine me. I cancelled the date immediately, taking a trick from John and blocking his number from my phone, and tried to forget what might have been.

Having not had much luck with the men of the online dating world, I decide to try a new tactic for meeting a match. I think I've been too creative in my choices of males, choosing intrigue and adventure, a method that has seemed to end in disaster each time, and decide that maybe I should err on the side of sensible and reliable instead. I look at some of the men I respect most in my life: my dad, my uncle, my best friend's husband – and I realise they have a few traits in common. They're good decent men with solid responsible jobs, loving partners who work hard for their families both emotionally and career-wise. *Forget the bad boys*, think I, *that sounds like a sensible angle to play this singles game from.*

Actively searching out stability and dependability is how I meet my next date, Nick. Unusually, as my usual trick is to favour an older man, Nick is two years younger than me, but I excuse him for his age by the fact he is 6 foot 3: almost the perfect height. The slightly awkward images in his online dating profile don't set my loins on fire (I mentally add 'quirky Christmas jumpers' to my list of virtual turn-offs) but the fact that he's intelligent – he's a solicitor – and has no cringy steroid-sponsored gym pics or dodgy urinal selfies just about sells his profile to me.

The children are left being looked after by my parents one Sunday while I go to meet him for a drink at a local pub. It's a pleasant meeting; we chat generally over a couple of lemonades – but I don't feel a spark and leave feeling slightly despondent, wondering if my tactic of searching out Mr Practical means I will also have to settle for Mr Slightly Boring. Having made a conscious rational decision to eschew the bad boys in exchange for ordinary Nick, I'm disappointed that I found him more snoozeworthy than sensible. He was wearing a nice shirt, I'll give him that, and as he was the only man who hadn't blocked me on WhatsApp in the last three months (along with his good height), I thought I should give him another chance.

I next see him on a Friday night for a dinner date. I'm wearing a pair of sky-high Louboutins that I had treated myself to after finishing a long and arduous work project, and though I can't walk in the bastards I'm feeling at peak sexiness: the impending blister on my big toe gives me an impressive sashay, I think, as I limp across the restaurant to our table.

Nick sits opposite me sipping a beer, a nice Ralph Lauren shirt on his back and a dour expression on his face. I can tell this isn't going to be the most exciting date but I decide to buck myself up and make the most of it anyway, ordering a bottle of wine that, as it turns out, he doesn't want to share. Over the next couple of hours I do what all the magazine articles tell you you shouldn't when faced with a bit of a boring date: I drink until I'm so tipsy that his company becomes fun.

Sixty minutes and two glasses of wine later I'm finding Nick *hilarious*. Not only this but I have turned into the most glittering company myself: my jokes don't miss a beat, my tinkling laughter is coquettish, not tipsy (it's *definitely* tipsy). *If I were on a date with myself I'd be bowled over by what great company I am*, I think. I wobble into the bathroom to use the loo and redo my lipstick, flicking my hair at myself in the mirror. Wine should be a prerequisite for all dates, I stupidly think, as I strut back to my entirely unremarkable dinner partner, my alcohol buzz as big as my toe blister.

Everything post-dessert is a bit of a blur, and I wake up the next morning full of nausea and regret. Nick lies next to me, his hairy back a stark physical representation of exactly what I didn't want to do last night: take the man home with me. I vaguely remember some ill-advised espresso martinis at the table as well as a drink in the cocktail bar next door – was there some dancing involved? – and though I brought this unwanted visitor with me, I'm glad I made it home safely.

I feel under the sheets. Thankfully I'm still wearing my bra and knickers. With Nick still snoozing, I hop out of bed and loudly get dressed, making noises about how late it is (it's 8 a.m. on a Saturday, it's really not late) in the hope that it'll encourage him to leave. His exit isn't forthcoming, though, and in the end I offer to drive him the three miles home to get him out of my house. We finally leave together and I return home to wash my sheets, wash the man I didn't particularly like out of my house.

I'm not too keen on seeing Nick again, but one evening six weeks later, after a run of depressing Tinder messages from the single men of Milton Keynes, I decide to accept his offer of a Saturday dinner date. It's his birthday weekend, which should have been an indication of the kind of person he was – why wasn't he out celebrating the occasion with friends or family?

– but I mistakenly tell myself it's sweet that he'd like to spend the evening with me.

We eat sushi, a very lovely meal, and having learned a harsh lesson on our previous date I drink only one glass of wine. As we leave the restaurant for a post-dinner drink it starts to snow, making a glorious scene, one that I'd only seen before in Richard Curtis movies. I make an effusive comment about how beautifully romantic this is while he stoically keeps looking ahead, and despite being an eternal optimist I wonder how long I can keep my fixed smile plastered on my face without getting actually plastered.

Two gin and tonics later and I'm ready to go home. The snow is still coming down pretty heavily and, as it's early January, this is the last child-free opportunity I have to finish filling out my tax return (I know, I know, sexy date chat: I HAVE IT).

'OK,' he says, 'I'll get us a taxi.'

'Oh no, you misunderstand,' I say gently. 'I'm going home alone tonight.'

He looks shocked. 'Why?' he asks.

Unused to such a direct question when I've just implied to a date that I don't want to have sex with them, I don't really know what to say. 'Umm . . . I just want to,' I stumble. 'I want to go home on my own.'

'But that's not fair,' he counters, gesturing to his crotch. 'You just kissed me, I'm excited now. You can't send me home alone. I'm turned on, I need to come back with you.'

I can't quite believe my ears, the insistent way this man is telling me he somehow deserves to come back to my house and have sex with me, purely because we'd just had a quick and fumbling kiss. I don't know what else to say, so I just go with a firm 'No.'

He sighs. 'OK then,' he concedes, 'I'll come home with you and we'll only go to bed together. We can just lie there – I promise I won't try to have sex with you.'

Not believing that if I take him home he won't try to rub his grubby crotch all over me, I laugh. 'You've got to be kidding me?' I say. Seeing his stony face, I apologise when I really shouldn't: 'I'm sorry, but no.'

'FINE,' he says, physically scooting his body away and crossing his arms, his body language telling me he is incredibly annoyed. Again I feel – erroneously – at fault, despite this man I don't particularly like overtly trying to push me into letting him into my house, letting him into my bed.

'I'm just very tired,' I soothe, rubbing his arm, 'maybe next time?' Despite his shitty behaviour I hate upsetting him, and search for a way I might appease this awful man for the sex he's not getting tonight. 'Why don't we share a taxi home, we live close enough?'

We get in a car together and he gives me the silent treatment all the way back to my house, not looking at me as I hand him a tenner that will much more than cover my share of the taxi. 'Goodnight then,' I say as the cab pulls up. I walk to my front door and start to unlock it.

All of a sudden, I hear a car door slam behind me and turn round in surprise. Nick has appeared by my side. 'What are you doing?' I ask. 'I told you I don't want you here.'

'Please,' he says with pleading and desperate eyes, 'I need a drink of water.'

At this point I should have screamed, should have told him to bugger off, should have called the police, even. But I'm so shocked that this man, this seemingly mild-mannered sensible solicitor, has acted so monumentally terribly that I don't. I'm simply at a loss. If this situation happened to me now, slap bang in the era of #MeToo and #TimesUp, I definitely would have reacted in a completely different way, but at the start of my new-found dating life I still had this weird belief that women somehow owed men sex or intimacy when they asked for it. I *really* didn't want to give it to him that night, though, and I wouldn't.

Earlier that evening, in an uncharacteristic display of slovenliness, I'd left my hoover by the front door after cleaning, a massive Miele beast that, though it was the best vacuum I'd ever used, was a heavy nightmare to heft around the house. Now I thank whichever deity is in charge of these things that I'd run out of time to put it away before I'd gone out for dinner that night and, knowing it's there, as I open the front door I deftly step over it into my hallway. Turning back to the door, I move the hoover with my foot, using it to block Nick's entrance, causing him to step down off my front step. 'Wait there,' I say as I close and lock the front door.

Breathing deeply to try to steady my shaking hands, I go to the fridge and grab a bottle of water before returning to the man I've locked outside. I open the door slightly and thrust my arm through the small gap.

'Here you go,' I say, sticking the bottle unceremoniously in his hand. 'Have a nice night.' It's January, it's snowing, he doesn't have a proper coat and I don't care.

I close and lock the door once more, collapsing on the stairs and burying my head in my arms. I start to cry. Had I done a few things differently that night – drunk more, felt a little lonelier, been less romantically experienced or slightly younger – I would have definitely caved in to his demands, let him come home with me. I would have definitely ended up having sex with him against my will and that thought terrified me. How had my love life come to this? How, in 2015, were we in a place where men thought it OK to pressure women into having sex with them – to persist after they'd clearly been told 'NO'? I resolved never to do anything a man told me again.

The next day Nick texts me while I'm at the gym. 'I had to walk three miles home last night, you're cruel, LOL,' he says. Shocked and astounded, I don't reply.

I return to the text message later that day: 'Do you think it was a fun idea to try and coerce me into having sex with you?' I ask him.

He replies, 'It perhaps wasn't my finest hour ;) Do you want to go for a drink next week?'

'No. Never contact me again,' I tell him. Thankfully he doesn't.

One thing I'm always proud of (despite all my encounters with the men your mum warns you about) is the fact that, notwithstanding the nonsense, I still believe in love. I might have had a divorce, a terrible one-night stand and bad encounters with predators, cheaters and misogynists under my belt, but I am still hopeful that I will eventually find true love, will meet The One. Though to this concept of The One I say, F you Hollywood; you have a lot of broken dreams to answer for – there's a lot of women out there searching for perfection where it probably doesn't exist.

My quest for true love next takes me somewhere I don't expect to go. Somewhere I've been before, yep, but in a way that's completely unexpected and new to me. I go back to New York.

I decide to return there for my thirtieth birthday, a trip that is the absolute hugest treat to myself. I'm going back to meet my best friend Kate again but I'm doing it in style – and on my own worked-hard-for dollar. I've upgraded my own flights and booked a lovely room at Soho House, something that feels to me like the biggest achievement, and this fact is almost as exciting to me as the trip itself. I've gone from being a woman teetering on the edge of her own sanity to a single mother at twenty-seven, divorced the man I thought was the love of my life and have restarted what's turned out to be a pretty good career. I'm bankrolling my own holidays and my own life, and it feels absolutely brilliant.

I'm on a champagne-and-life high as I arrive at JFK, buzzing through immigration before hopping in one of those yellow cabs that so got my heart racing three years ago. We cross the East River as the sun sets and I head for my hotel in the Meatpacking District – I feel like I'm in a movie. I arrive and unpack, then take a quick stroll around the block to buy some bits from CVS (those huge American drugstores piss all over sensible Boots the Chemist, in my opinion: I mean, they sell *beer*), and after a speedy thirty-minute power nap and shower I'm ready to meet Kate for dinner at 8 p.m. I'm tired but determined to put my best face forward, knowing I've got only five precious days ahead of me in the Big Apple; I don't want to waste any of them on jet lag.

We catch up over burrata, squid and vodka martinis and I feel happy – I'm home. I'm here without a man but I don't care: I have a great friend by my side and the world at my feet. What could possibly go wrong? We finish up dinner slightly early but agree to meet for brunch the next day at SoHo's trendy Jack's Wife Freda and I head for bed at eleven, crashing immediately.

I'm up with the lark on Sunday, calling a sleepy Kate to discuss the arrangements for our brunch. She tells me she's invited another expat to join us, an old university friend of hers called Aiden, and I inwardly groan: I've come all this way to spend time with my BFF and I don't really want to share her company with a bloke I've never met; they'll no doubt share anecdotes of people I've neither met nor care about. 'Sounds great!' I trill to her, not meaning it one little bit but firmly deciding that negativity won't taint my holiday.

I've brought the London weather with me and despite it being July it's pissing it down. The dampness of the skies does not dampen my Brits Abroad spirit though; I feel right at home, and even though I'm slightly hungover from the plane champagne and previous night's cocktails I grab an umbrella and walk the couple of miles through the city to Carmine Street in SoHo. Kate's late – she's always late – so I stop off in a neighbouring Starbucks for a coffee. A bloke on the table next to me asks me to watch his MacBook while he nips to the loo and I'm proud: I reckon he must have mistaken me for an actual New Yorker if he's trusting me with his Apple products.

She arrives and rages at me for a couple of seconds for not 'booking in' with the hostess (I must have missed the 'how to do brunch' lesson in my *Sex and the City* education about New

York) and we hang around outside the restaurant for a few more minutes waiting for Aiden to arrive. He bowls up in an Uber and introduces himself, saying something incomprehensible about getting in at 4 a.m. that morning after a wild night. Our table is ready so I roll my eyes, say 'Shall we?' and we step in to brunch.

Aiden – if you haven't already guessed it – is my next big love interest. It comes from absolutely nowhere, punching me square in the nose during a fight I didn't even know I was in. I had expectations of New York only of wonderful times with my good friend; I hadn't wanted to involve any men in the equation. The situation I find myself in with him catches me completely unawares, but once it does, I'm hooked.

It takes me a while to warm to Aiden. He's what the Americans would describe as a 'goof' and the British a 'cheeky chappy'. He's three years older than me and has moved over to New York City to pursue a career in sports marketing, following a dream he's always had to live abroad (via London and Manchester). He's funny and the three of us have a rip-roaring laugh over our brunch, moving on from Jack's Wife Freda to drink jugs of watermelon margaritas at a Mexican cafe with huge open windows looking out on the wet SoHo streets.

I don't know when my attraction to him starts but all of a sudden there it is: somewhere in between the margaritas and a rooftop gin and tonic at the Jane Hotel overlooking the Statue of Liberty, a whole school laboratory full of chemistry suddenly appears and a full-on lady boner pops up in my pants. A tourist snaps an iPhone photo for our tipsy threesome and I send it to a friend later for 'What do you think of this hottie?' opinions – she tells me the attraction is so palpable in the photograph that she

185

thought we'd already consummated our fledgling flirtatious relationship. Looking at the image with fresh eyes I indeed recognise that I look like I'm about to drop trou and hump his leg (I didn't. I promise).

A group of us go to dinner that evening and, playing it cooler than a well-iced cucumber, I pretend to not be thrilled when Aiden takes the seat next to mine. He makes me laugh, something that's always been so important when it comes to the men I'm attracted to, and this fact alongside the pulse of the city I love renders me completely intoxicated.

I've never had a holiday romance before but a love interest in New York seems much more appealing than a couple of quick shags on the beach in Faliraki, so I go with it. Aiden and I see each other every single day after he's finished work for the rest of my trip and, as my time in the city draws to a close, I start to wonder what will happen after I leave. He and I are having so much fun together that the thought of it coming to an end prematurely makes me feel incredibly sad. Which is why, one evening, I tentatively ask him if he thinks we should see each other again, a pretty loaded question from someone who lives three and a half thousand miles away.

'I can't imagine not seeing you again,' he says to me, and that's it. I book my return flight at the airport, even as I sniffle after a sad goodbye.

I was back five weeks later and this time Aiden had taken the week off work to spend with me. He greeted me at the front door of his apartment in the East Village with a bottle of champagne and a massive smile: we sat on the roof of the building and watched the sun set behind the Empire State Building while we drank and chatted and drank and chatted. I felt like I was in heaven, touristing with him like no other tourist ever has before, taking in museums, art exhibitions, endless walks and many more rooftops. I spent the days in a perpetual state of feeling like I was in a movie or a dream, waking up to the most incredible New York vistas and spending my days hailing yellow cabs and dodging those Marilyn Monroe-esque pavement (sorry, 'sidewalk') steam vents. I was Carrie Bradshaw, if Carrie Bradshaw lived in Milton Keynes and only took the odd sojourn out to the Big Apple.

I visited New York to see Aiden for four consecutive months, and as I started planning my fifth visit I felt the tide change. I'd normally have a couple of days of emotional text messaging to regroup after I touched down in London, waiting for the jet lag and the heartbreak of leaving the man I liked and the city I loved to dissipate, but this time Aiden just wasn't warm. Text messages would go un-replied to, phone calls were unanswered. Knowing he was going through a difficult time at work, I felt terrible for him, recognising the stress he was under; his visa was directly tied to his job, if he lost it he'd only have six weeks to leave a country he loved. Though we weren't labelling each other boyfriend and girlfriend, I wanted to do everything I could to play the role of supportive female lead in his life, so I kept on caring and calling for far longer than the incommunicative arsehole deserved.

I could have just taken the fact that Aiden stopped communicating with me as a hint that he didn't want to see me any more. I could have taken it lying down. But, with John the Media

Mogul's swift ignore-and-block and Nick's predatory behaviour still raw in my mind, I didn't want to. What I wanted to do was go and visit the city I loved once more and ask Aiden what he was playing at, why he'd gone from so hot to so cold in such a short amount of time.

And so I did.

Hearing about my pickle, my Australian friend Chris (who was coincidentally going to be in the city at the same time) invited me to a wedding he was attending in Connecticut, and I couldn't imagine anything I'd like to do more to help me forget about Aiden. I'd fly to JFK and take a town car out to the American version of Buckinghamshire, where I'd indulge in cocktail hour and dance til my feet bled: what could be more perfect? Once more, finding myself in New England in the 'fall', in the midst of all these people who grew up in places like 'the Midwest' and California, I felt like I was in a movie. God, I loved America.

Chris and I took a car into the city the next day. I dropped my bags at my hotel and him at his apartment before he took me on a pushbike-based crawl of the best sports bars in New York. We drank beer and ate chicken wings, and he listened as I cried over my failing transatlantic romance with Aiden, playing his role of supportive friend incredibly well.

Speaking of the incommunicative bastard, as I was now referring to him, he phoned me as Chris and I were out to dinner that evening. He was very sorry for not being in touch sooner, he said. He'd been out of town but he'd love to see me: could we meet up tomorrow?

And meet up we did, chatting around our situation until he finally admitted that he felt terrible with his work situation in so much flux. I was heartbroken for him, sad that he hadn't felt able to talk more to me about exactly how hard he'd been finding the work situation. I wanted to make everything seem OK, wanted to make it all OK for him.

We went back to my hotel together and he left early the next morning, telling me he had a Labor Day trip to a farm in the Hamptons planned with some colleagues. We said our goodbyes and I prepared to fly home later that day knowing something still wasn't quite right. Despite his protestations, I knew it wasn't just work.

Later that day I woefully scroll through Instagram at the airport as I wait for my flight, and spot a photograph Aiden has uploaded of a smack-in-the-face seasonal cart of pumpkins, tagged with a location somewhere near a place called Mattituck, NY. Feeling despondent, I click on the name of the farm, perusing other users' images, getting more and more annoyed at the happy faces of the people who are having fun with the person I should be hanging out with.

My thumb stops mid-scroll as I see a name I've seen before: Deanna. I look a bit closer. Aiden had liked Deanna's farm photograph, the matching cart of matching sodding pumpkins.

I didn't know a Deanna: I'd met most of Aiden's New York-based friends by then, or at the very least had heard stories of the ones he regularly hung out with. My mind went back to a fleeting memory of where I'd seen the name before. It was only once before, a couple of months ago.

I had, as usual, flown to JFK on the Virgin Atlantic flight that got in just as he finished work. I'd rushed to his apartment, offering to pick up the sheets held hostage at his local laundro-mat, the ones he'd taken in to be washed that morning. He'd left his key with his doorman and I'd let myself into the flat, unpack-ing my stuff and making the bed like a good non-girlfriend for him to come home to later. I'd got changed myself and rushed out to meet him at the gig we'd be going to that night as he rushed back from an upstate event he was hosting.

We had our reunion outside the front of Terminal 5, a Hell's Kitchen music venue where the Kills were playing that night (I know, I went all the way to New York to see a London band: I'm an idiot). Excited to see each other again – or so I thought – we'd hurried inside the club, where the band's set had already started.

As we stood at the bar to order drinks, Aiden's phone, laid out in front of him, lit up with the arrival of a text message. Despite my internet research skills I'm not really one to snoop on a part-ner's phone but, as I reckon any of us (amateur sleuths or not) would do when faced with a blinking light, I automatically looked at the screen. It was a text from a Deanna.

'Hope you have an amazing night! Xx,' it said.

Noting the familiar tone as well as the double kiss – some-thing I've been told doesn't come as an automatic sign-off for Americans as it does us overly effusive Brits – I filed it away, deep in my 'things to forget about because nobody wants to be with the girl who stresses over every female interaction' file. And there it had remained, until now.

I look at the next photograph on Aiden's Instagram feed, a photograph I'd taken of him in his bedroom, wearing his favour-ite T-shirt. She'd liked that image too. I check to see how long they'd been friends on the platform; it was after we'd met but at least a month ago.

I fly home feeling absolutely gutted. Everything had started coming together like a particularly hideous and nauseating jigsaw: was the reason Aiden was so keen on washing his sheets before I arrived on my last trip because she'd slept in them the previous night? When I called him all those times and he didn't answer, was it because he was on dates with her? Why couldn't he just come clean about the situation that was as sordid as his sheets?

Predictably, he swerved my calls all the next week, claiming a sore throat and flu as the reason for his absence. I knew this was all, as the Americans like to say, absolute bullshit; as soon as I saw another photo of him and her on Instagram at Sleep No More, an immersive theatrical experience we'd talked about attending together, I knew they were boning. And there they were again on Deanna's Instagram but this time as a couple, a lipstick mark on his forehead (the caption: 'We're so cute!', vomit), him playing drunken *Guitar Hero* in her kitchen, those pumpkins they picked together carved on his dining table. I felt sick.

It took ten days before I finally got him on the phone, and thankfully (for him, at least) by the time we spoke I was less upset and more incandescently fuming with rage. With our locations so far apart, I hadn't been under any illusions about our extended holiday romance being some kind of long-lasting love story, but, once again, I was so sad and disappointed that someone had treated me in a way I felt was so disrespectful, so unrepresentative of our lovely times.

'Just tell me if you don't want to be with me any more!' I wanted to scream. 'I'm a big girl, I can take it.' It was almost a relief to hear him cop to the fact that he'd met someone else (screw you, Deanna) and that yes, he and I were over.

In what was a total shock to the system, I took this break-up harder than my divorce. I spent more time than I'd like to admit stalking both of their Instagrams, watching as they moved in together, rolling my eyes at photographs of her in the bed I've slept in, hanging out with the friends I've spent time with. If this wasn't the 'Information Age' and I was doing all this in real life rather than over an app I'd be a bona fide mentalist.

Aiden emailed me a couple of months later to let me know that he'd lost his job and that he was marrying Deanna. I was gutted; yet another man I'd mooned over had been able to move on as quick as a flash, returning to their life without me as if our relationship had never happened. And not only returning to his life, forming a new one with someone else. I had put his shitty behaviour partly down to his being a footloose and fancy-free bachelor living the high life in New York, but his impending marriage well and truly put paid to my pie-in-the-sky theories. Once again I was stuck in my past while everyone else got on with life.

I felt like I'd spent the three years preceding my New York affair in a life of dogged solo parenting, persistently pushing to succeed in a life I'd never ordered but had found served up like a Shake Shack burger: one layered not with gherkins and deliciously plastic cheese but with despondency, loneliness and work worries. Having Aiden to retreat to in New York had made me feel so exotic in a world where I'd spent a long time feeling like I was on the bottom rung of society, the single mother left to rot in a pool of her own bad decision-making.

I wouldn't miss Aiden as much as I would miss the incredible excitement that New York had brought to my life: it was a safe haven where I could retreat away from the persona – the single-mum one – that I was still almost afraid and ashamed of. Returning to a New York-less life meant settling once again for the drudgery of everyday school runs, packed lunches and PTA meetings. In one fell swoop I'd gone from Carrie Bradshaw to Josephine Bloggs, from New York back to Milton Keynes.

I'd completely rebelled against the label of single mother when I first became one, wanting anything but to be lumped in with society's failures, a disaster in marriage, a drain on resources. I wanted something better for me and my family and for a short while my trips abroad had given me that; they'd given me the excitement and sophistication that I'd so craved outside of my little mum bubble. And I was absolutely gutted the trans-atlantic adventure was over.

I was back to earth, back to my life, with an almighty, unpleasant bang.

CHAPTER THIRTEEN

The Single Parent Life

I wish I could say that was it when it came to the excitement of my dating life but it wasn't. I continued to be confused by the pure weirdness of the thirty- and forty-something single men I was meeting who, it turned out, were most definitely single for a reason.

There's the TV comedian I dated for three months, a man who has somehow got to the age of thirty-two without eating an avocado (quite the achievement for a millennial) and whose strict Irish Catholic upbringing has led to some pretty weird ideas about sex, including him thinking it's 'fun' to pin me down and lick my face and never let a naked body be seen in daylight.

Then there's the twenty-six-year-old ex-professional athlete who doesn't have much to say but looks *very* good naked. The conversation peters out after four weeks: I'd like to say it was good while it lasted but it really wasn't.

After that is the five months I spend with Mark, a forty-eight-year-old American whose *joie de vivre* after getting out of a difficult marriage is almost infectious. As he lives in London we don't get the opportunity to see each other more than once or twice a week, and we break up on a holiday in Greece. Three days into the break. It's awkward.

I have an on/off thing with my (male, straight) hairdresser for a while, a situation that makes my styling appointments a lot more exhilarating than usual, but that quickly fizzles out when he gets a girlfriend who works at Soho House and who is therefore way cooler than little old me, the Single Mum from Milton Keynes.

I'm then ghosted by a man I mistakenly think is a good match: he works as a Formula One team manager, perfect for me because he's travelling 70 per cent of the time and is therefore not going to want to hang out at my house having me cook him dinner, as many men do (I swear eight out of ten blokes in their thirties are looking to marry their mum). After three months – and an invitation to his sister's wedding – Formula One man stands me up for a date and never calls me again, behaviour that – you guessed it! – leaves me fuming. Luckily, this time there isn't an ocean between my anger and the man who has seemingly disappeared off the face of the earth, and one happy Saturday about a month after his vanishing act I bump into him at the shopping centre. I ask him what on earth happened and he hops up and down on the spot awkwardly like a toddler needing a wee, bumbling through excuses about how he couldn't contact me because he was having a busy time at work. 'You look pretty,' he says to me on that day, the day I'm hopped up on adrenaline and the general man-related rage that I thought I'd forgotten about.

'I KNOW,' I say as I turn on my heel and walk away. As Beyoncé would say, 'Boy-bye.'

In between my dazzling new identities as a career woman and serial dater (read: knackered workaholic and disappointed Tinder user) I try to find my feet in the one job that matters the most: the single mother. Having been pretty dependent on my husband – practically and emotionally – ever since I met him as a teenager, this is the most daunting role I've ever taken on. And, as I did lots of amateur dramatics when I was younger – actual singing and tap dancing on a stage, not a euphemism for throwing a tantrum – that's saying something.

At first I'm incredibly ashamed of being a single parent and, though with hindsight I realise this wasn't the case, I feel negatively judged at every turn, every baby group, every coffee morning. Showing up at the John Lewis cafe for the tea and cake bought by my loyalty vouchers (Mama's on one income now, folks) with a small baby and toddler in tow, I'm convinced the elderly customers are whispering about me behind their pension books, talking about the poor children with the unmarried mother, the woman whose wedding ring is conspicuous by its absence.

It takes about three years of single parent slog for my mindset to come round to the fact this is my life now, there's no husband nor long-term prospective partner on the horizon, and this is OK. It doesn't happen overnight, it's a slow process, but I gradually start to realise that I should be proud of where I am and where I've come from. I don't know if it's the fact that I'm paying rent, making money and raising my kids by myself, save for every other weekend when they're with their dad, but I'm comfortable with doing it solo, and I stop believing that I need a man to validate me or make me whole.

I still think about that ridiculous belief now, the one that tells us we're not complete unless we have a partner. I roll my eyes every time I hear someone refer to their husband or wife as their 'other half': are you not complete without them? No! It's a cute idea, that we all have this one person we simply must navigate life with to make it meaningful, but I can tell you now it's not accurate: life is also bloody great when you're doing it solo.

The logistics of trying to hold down a job while parenting kids alone aside (nurseries, school timetables and children's sick days not being conducive to working back-breaking hours in advertising), it proves fairly easy for my little family of three to get into a routine. I realise how much of a housewife role I'd taken on in my old marriage: cooking all the food, doing all the washing, playing cleaner and caretaker. With no adult-sized pants to pick up off the floor (apart from my own . . . though I seem to have no problem reaching the washing bin) and no man-sized egos to take care of, looking after just two children and myself is comparatively a breeze. Though day-to-day organisation is more difficult – there's a reason why I'm the most anally tidy person on the planet, and it's because if I wasn't then none of us would get out of the front door in the morning – the emotional labour I used to suffer under is all but gone. Yes, if I want things done I either have to do them myself or pay someone more capable at brandishing a drill than I, but this removal of pressure that comes with no longer expecting someone else to do jobs or tasks that you then have to nag them to complete – it's liberating.

The Single Parent Life

In my married house there was a definite split between boy jobs and girl jobs. Almost everything related to the kids or home would be my domain – roles I reckon we naturally fell into as a couple thanks to our traditional upbringings; we both had stay-at-home mothers who spent our childhoods looking after the family homes and the breadwinning men in them. But these roles don't work when both people are working; granted, Will was toiling outside the home at his new business and I was doing a small amount of freelance work from the kitchen table, but I found the pressure of being expected to look after everything home-wise exhausting and overwhelming, especially when I was simultaneously trying to conquer my post-natal depression, look after the house and raise two children. I saw a fellow working mum say recently about her husband, who shares the jobs around the house more equally: 'If he doesn't wash his pants, he has no clean pants to wear' – this wasn't the situation in our house. I *always* washed the pants. I used to long for a day when I didn't wash those bloody pants.

Will often returned home to a wife who nagged him, a wife who required bins taking out, DIY completing, mess moved. He'd have been at work for ten hours and would want to sit down with a beer and his emails, but when I'd been at home staring at an IKEA shelf and an overflowing Brabantia all day, I just wanted him to get on with the jobs already: yes, I could do them myself, but I would be too tired in an evening to start learning how to use a power drill and I can't bear the smell of bloody bin juice, particularly when I had two kids in nappies. I hated being accused of nagging, he hated being nagged . . . it was a vicious circle of whining, nagging and frustration, and that was before you took the kids' tears into consideration. Which really didn't help us to lead the harmonious home life that Hollywood promised me.

As a single mum one of the things I miss most about having another body in the house is the sheer convenience of being able to get essentials from the shops at will. Got to bedtime and realise you've used the last of the milk? Ring your husband and ask him to pick it up on the way home. In your PJs already and fancy a Saturday-night bar of chocolate? Beg and plead the father of your children to pop to the Co-op and get you one. Yep, coming to terms with the death of convenience in my house was a difficult one.

It's embarrassing for me to admit how many times I've called my local fish and chip shop in tears, asking them where the humanity is in their refusal to implement a delivery system when this knackered single mum with sleeping kids is hungry, and only a pile of greasy potatoes and fish will do. I may have even, on one occasion, piled said sleeping kids into the car because of my extreme need for the grease. Desperate times, I tell you.

The day Deliveroo comes to Milton Keynes is a happy one for us all. OK, so they won't fetch and carry from Willen Fish Bar (to this day, the best fish and chips around), but a whole new world of at-home food purchasing has arrived on our doorstep. We have Byron! Wagamama! Pizza Express! And all in the comfort of our own PJs: it's wonderful, though the pounds I spend on the app quickly re-route themselves to my rear. I care not; what's a wobbly bottom when you can get yakisoba delivered to your door in forty-five minutes or less? It's calorie-heavy heaven.

I miss Will at the most twice a day. Once in the mornings, when I have to get the kids out of bed – Elfie's an early riser; she'd be up at 5 a.m. every day if I let her, whereas I will happily not speak until I've had three cups of tea or the clock hits 10 a.m., whichever comes later – and again in the evenings, when I would quite like someone to watch Netflix with me. I tackle these issues the only way I know how, and start to let Elfie come into bed with me alongside a pile of books (the iPad at the weekend) until I am ready to open my eyes and the curtains. Evening-wise I develop terrible taste in Netflix, watching shows I know every single straight man on the planet would hate: I've seen every franchise of *The Real Housewives* available and, when I exhaust these, I watch the less bad TV shows over and over, knowing no bloke would stand for such repetitive behaviour. To this day I know each episode of *Grey's Anatomy*, *The Good Wife* and *Girls* off by heart, wearing my obsession for my favourite programmes like one of the blankets on my sofa.

In the bigger scheme of things, I enjoy being solo again and discover a part of myself that I had no idea was missing. I realise that when married I acquiesed to my husband constantly; as he was the breadwinner I put his social and work needs above my own, asking for his permission to see friends or to take time away from the children to do things I wanted to do. Looking back I can see that this wasn't something he imposed on me; he wasn't the kind of person to tell me that I wasn't 'allowed' to see my friends or attend work events. The process of me asking him permission to go to the pub, asking him to be home by seven so I could make it out to see my local friends – this was something I introduced to the relationship and he complicitly went along with, telling me 'no' or 'yes' (and, with a business he needed to grow, it was often 'no'). Living as we did in a new area I quickly felt isolated, lost without the ability (by which I mean without a husband at home to look after the children) to venture out to the pub or a friend's house.

Around this time I started to notice my child-free friends distancing themselves, too. I had a massive chip on my shoulder when it came to asking if they wanted to spend time with me: with a husband rarely at home I found it hard to leave the house and I worried that they'd dislike me constantly requesting they come over to mine to see me. I didn't want them to feel like their world should suddenly start revolving around me, their friend who had got knocked up expecting them to fall in line with my new life. My cousins, who I adored, lived in the next town, but I was paranoid about always expecting them to come to my house if we were to see each other socially. I was a prisoner in my own home, tied to my kids and husband with invisible shackles that I'd fastened for myself, but didn't know how to undo.

When I become single I realise that I'd turned into a person who let herself be dictated to by a man, just because she was working inside the home instead of outside of it. I hate the fact that, when I used our joint account, I felt like I was spending 'his' money instead of 'our' money. I recognise just how much I despised feeling that Will was somehow a more important part of our relationship than I was because he was bringing home the bacon, even though I was working just as hard (and actually, sometimes harder: my job was 24/7) to raise our children. I wonder who the fuck I have become and, looking around me at the strong women I have befriended, realise I can't be this person any more.

Why shouldn't I feel as valid as the man in my house whose children I have birthed and who have cracked my nipples until they bleed? Why should I expect to be the one in the marriage equation who earns less and leaves her job at the drop of a hat to tend to offspring? Why should I ask permission to pop out of an evening to socialise?

Through my experiences of single-parenting I quickly realise how absolutely screwed women are when it comes to parenting as it relates to work. In my advertising career I am belittled; I am judged (behind my back, out loud and to my face) on my looks; I am asked, even when there are male junior colleagues present, to take minutes in meetings (despite having never taken minutes in my career); I am assumed to be a secretary because of my gender; I am expected to pander to male clients in the manner of a geisha (can I pour you some tea . . . ughh). All behaviour I have always taken as normal and acceptable. Until I realise it's not.

I've never obsessively watched *Keeping Up With The Kardashians* – that's one trashy TV show too far, even for me – but now I start to realise how right Kris Jenner has it. When it comes to both work and home lives, why shouldn't we take on the role of matriarch, dictating what happens to us, when it'll happen and how we'll do it? Why shouldn't we expect the same freedom, the same rights and roles, as men? Quite frankly, it's bloody ridiculous that we think it's OK to accept any less than equality. The realisation revolutionises the way I feel about my life, my work, my kids: everything.

I spend a few months bristling at the unjustness of life around me, realising how seamlessly complicit I am and the women I know are when it comes to falling in behind the wants and needs of men, whether that's our husbands or our colleagues. The other shoe finally drops: I'm a feminist.

It soon seems mad to me that I've never explored the concept of feminism before, particularly when I'm raising my children in a world where the gender pay gap, poor parliamentary and board representation, domestic violence, harassment and rape are such huge issues. How could I have thought this was OK? Learning about feminism while also unravelling how capable and resilient I actually am through my experience of divorce, I resolve to bring my kids up to expect no less than equality and the knowledge that they can be whoever they want to be, and this makes me feel so empowered in the rest of my life. Out of all the valuable personality traits single-parenting has brought me – resilience, openness, selflessness, perseverance – feminism is one of the most important ones, the one I hold most dear and will continue to pursue for the rest of my life. Where I'd once feared that I couldn't cope on my own, I suddenly know that I can. Where I'd worried I wouldn't be enough for my children, now I know that I am. And where I'd thought I needed a man by my side to feel validated, now I know I don't. I feel like I can fly!

But I can't, obviously. So I do the next best thing and get on a plane: I take my kids on holiday. Alone.

The children have been abroad before, to Madrid for my sister-in-law's wedding when they were six weeks and twenty-three months old. Back then I had a husband to be another pair of hands alongside relatives – sisters-in-law, aunties, my husband's mother

– to help. I wouldn't say it was a breeze but it wasn't horrendous, and I even managed the odd glass of wine in the sunshine.

But I knew that taking my two out of the country alone would be a whole other struggle, and that's before I factored in Elfie's medical condition and the catalogue of medications and syringes I'd need to carry through the airport. Travel stress for the win!! Or the wine? Either way, it was a mountain I'd have to climb eventually, and I desperately wanted to remember how it felt to get on a plane and go somewhere nice; and even more than that, I wanted to give the feeling of sunshine and freedom to my kids.

In all my years of parenting solo I've had a fair few queries that go along the lines of 'How on earth do you do it?' They're normally prefaced with anecdotes like, 'My husband was away on business for three days last week and I lost my mind . . .' or, 'I hate flying even when there's an extra pair of hands to help with the kids, I can't imagine doing it alone . . .' The thing is, situations always look hard unless you're slap bang in the middle of them. Even I, the person who's been through the mill a fair bit when it comes to solo parenting – living alone in an unfamiliar place with a six-month-old and two-year-old was not easy – look at parents of newborns, just new parents, not even single mothers, and think 'Fuck me, that looks tough.' Because it is – the situations we're in are all tough and all relative. Back when I was twenty-three I found going to work every single day difficult because I wasn't used to it, but as I got on with it the forty-hour work week became my new normal. The same happened in my life as a single mum.

As in all situations, whether we're a new mum or single parent, the answer is that we just do it, we just get on with it. And it's true in every facet in life, whether you're struggling with your very first job in your early twenties, giving birth for the first time at thirty or becoming a single mum at twenty-seven. You just buckle up, knuckle down and do what you have to do; and that's also true when it comes to travelling with children.

Our first single-parent holiday was to a Mark Warner resort in Greece and it was epically brilliant. I chose the resort because of the company's excellent reputation for childcare, and the fact that our package included three hours of activities for the children each day, plus evening babysitting if I so required. I knew that taking them away solo would be intense, so I wanted to make sure I had the option of precious time alone to, you know, read a book or stare mutely at my feet, whichever took my fancy.

We arrived at the resort after a surprisingly pleasant flight. I'd packed like a ninja, making sure the children had the responsibility of their own Trunkis so I wouldn't be left hefting everyone's clothes through the airport; and, despite Hux crashing into a few fellow travellers' ankles with his suitcase-on-wheels, the journey was pretty drama-free. I admittedly felt conscious of my single status on the plane, a charter flight that seemed to be full only of nuclear families, but that was soon forgotten as we arrived in Greece.

Despite finding the organised-fun aspect of the holiday a bit cringy on arrival, we soon got into the swing of it. The resort felt to me like the holiday version of John Lewis, a safe place full of nice people (or am I the only person who gets that vibe from a department store? Perhaps don't answer that question). I felt incredibly awkward at the start making conversation with strangers, but soon got used to it and became pally with the parents of the kids my own children were spending time with; we even began our own nightly routine of a 7 p.m. cocktail hour as the sun set over the beach.

The kids adored the trip, splitting their time between wind-surfing, swimming, beach games and ice creams. I felt more relaxed than I had in years and even read a whole book, something I hadn't done for as long as I could remember. We returned to the UK rested and rejuvenated and I vowed to make the effort to go abroad every year.

Because I like a challenge, or perhaps because I am a glutton for travel-shaped punishment, the next holiday we embarked on as a one-parent family was a ski trip. I'd learned the sport when I was a teenager and, although I wasn't hugely keen on any kind of physical activity (particularly when supposed to be enjoying a 'relaxing' holiday), I decided it would be character-building for my kids to experience the slopes.

I don't know if you've ever been on a ski holiday, but to keep dry and warm in the snow you need an amount of clothing that is almost comical. Each child had their trusty Trunki packed to the gills with massive ski jackets and salopettes, accompanied by ski socks, under-layers, ski goggles and assorted general cosy paraphernalia. As the only adult in the group I took the brunt of the packing and somehow towed two suitcases along with me, one of which could only be described as fucking massive.

We stay at Gatwick the night before our flight to minimise stress the next morning, waking at 4 a.m. for our 7 a.m. flight. I expect the kids to happily rise and shine with my (annoying) cries of 'WE'RE GOING ON HOLIDAAAAAAYYYY!!!', but both children are Eeyore levels of grumpy, batting away my attempts to wake them up with actual punches and little child-sized growls. Whatever; feeling as faux-chirpy as Maria from *The Sound of Music*, I somehow manage to get us all to check-in with loads of time and hurry them along to a restaurant where I promise them a lovely breakfast.

We sit across from each other at the restaurant table; well, I sit across from Elfie while poor sleepy Hux tries his hardest to snooze back off in my lap as I run through the options of what we might like to order. It's avocado toast for me, porridge for Hux and pancakes for Elfie, and I try to encourage my sleepy twosome to get stuck into the kids' menu colouring-in as we wait, which is always a battle even when we're not facing an ungodly hour of the morning. Our food arrives and we all stare blankly at it, none of us hungry (why did I think 5 a.m. was a good time to try to force-feed my children their breakfast?). I have a couple of token mouthfuls of my toast because I'm the mum and therefore it's my job to try to set a good example.

After not really eating anything, we take off for our gate, all ready to board the 7 a.m. to Grenoble. Only there are two 7 a.m. flights to Grenoble, and once we get in the queue to board I realise we're at the wrong 7 a.m. flight to Grenoble. It's 6.45 a.m. and we're on the opposite side of the airport to where we should be, a gate that's a good twenty-minute walk away from where we're currently queueing.

I let out a string of expletives that would be suited to Hugh Grant in *Four Weddings*, if only Hugh Grant's character had small children who weren't used to hearing their parent swear: 'Flip flip flip flip flip SUGAR.'

'Kids, we need to run,' say I, grabbing a tired hand in each of mine and taking off.

To save space in our suitcases I'd made each child wear their ski jacket and snow boots, and all of us (including me) are toting a backpack full of plane and holiday activities. It's an uncomfortably sweaty sprint across the departures hall and down those endless spidery corridors with gates leading off them, the slow people milling around us seemingly constantly in our way. Hux gives up on our athletic efforts and starts crying, something I quite fancy doing as well, so I heave him into my arms and Elfie and I resume our hot and sticky running.

By some kind of miracle we make it to our gate five minutes before the plane is due to take off. We're so late that we're the last people to board, but not late enough that the other passengers applaud us: I take that as a success and collapse, on the brink of a heart attack, into my zero-legroom seat.

I'd like to say the rest of the holiday is uneventful but it really isn't. It's simply really bloody hard to coordinate two young children and an adult on a ski holiday on your own. The juggle begins on arrival at our destination airport, where of course there are no luggage trolleys to be found and so I have to beg six-year-old Elfie to drag one of the large suitcases behind her while I hoist a Trunki on the back of the biggest case. We make it, though, and after both kids spend our two-hour coach transfer sleeping (score!!) we head out for lunch in the most beautiful spot we've ever visited together: two twenty-euro pizzas for them and a five-euro beer for me (I'd earned it).

Later that afternoon, after I try (and fail) to get the kids to take another nap, we head out of our chalet-hotel to pick up the ski gear I've pre-booked and paid for. This is the easy bit: getting the equipment back half a mile to the hotel is not. We've got skis for each of us, plus ski boots, helmets and poles, and the children are having too much fun charging through the snow to have any interest in carrying their own stuff. I could cry, lugging all those things back to the hotel myself: I have not wished for a husband more since the early days of my divorce.

Getting each child up, fed and dressed in their ski outfits ready for their mornings in ski school by 8.30 a.m. each and every day is an incredible feat of organisation that requires us to get up at 6.30 a.m., sometimes a tough time to rise after an evening on the Alps' best red wine. I feel so proud and accomplished to see my two snow bunnies shuffle off for their lessons each morning, knowing we are there in the magical mountain snow because of my hard work, perseverance and sheer organisation. And they love it, love their lessons on the slopes, love the time with their new friends building snowmen and throwing snowballs. Though I grow muscles this holiday from hefting so much equipment around, the week is one of the most special we've ever spent together.

We get up at 4 a.m. again for our coach transfer home, and because I am thinking about the couple of hours of sleep I might be able to snatch in the transfer before we get to the airport I blindly agree to the kids sitting on the back seat. And so we resume our journey back down the mountains, the children and I bounce-bounce-bouncing our way towards Grenoble.

'Mummy, I feel sick,' says Elfie before promptly throwing up on my lap and hers. I clean us both up as best as I can with the pack of baby wipes the mother in front of us has kindly handed to me, resolving to always from now on choose the seats at the front when I'm descending mountains with the kids.

The plane is delayed by two hours, a trial that would have been much more bearable had we not all risen at 4 a.m. and if we didn't smell faintly of vomit. But finally we take off, and I say a little prayer of thanks that we'll be back home soon.

The first time I travelled abroad on my own with the kids I crossed all the Ts and dotted all the Is when it came to our paperwork: I'd changed my married surname back to my maiden name soon after the split, feeling like a fraud having Will's surname instead of my own. Therefore the children and I no longer shared a name and I was terrified I might be pulled aside for this at immigration. So, for our first holiday, I asked Will to write a letter granting the children permission to be out of the country with me, as is protocol for separated families.

But as the parent with major custody this pissed me off no end. *Why should I have to ask my ex-husband's permission to leave the country with my own children?* I wondered. In the five years we'd been separated he'd never taken then abroad, and it stung that they were with me the majority of the time, our holidays were something I toiled hard for, yet I was still the one having to bend to these ridiculous misogynistic rules.

And so every holiday since I have refused to take such a permission letter with me, travelling only with a copy of the kids' birth certificates, my old marriage certificate and my certified deed poll. I'd never been questioned by Border Control, but knew that if they tried it I would have ready my answers to their difficult questions, and be able to shame them for daring to query the parentage of the children I worked hard to take on holiday.

Not this time, though.

Carting my vomit-soaked self through Gatwick that morning, I wasn't prepared to be quizzed on whether or not I was the mother of my children.

'Can you tell me the dates of birth of your children, please?' said the woman at the counter.

'Of course – 14 May,' said I, pointing at Hux and giving my ex-husband's birthday. 'And 25 July,' I stated, gesturing at Elfie as I told her my own. 'Oh hang on, that might be wrong,' I went on, smiling nervously. 'It was a very early morning!' I tried again, and thankfully got their birthdays right this time.

'And where were they born?' the border official asked.

'Oh gosh, I know this one!' I said. 'I was there after all! Hahah! Er . . . right. One was Nottingham and one was Milton Keynes.'

By some miracle – I'm sure it was down to the fact that Elfie bears more than a striking resemblance to me (or possibly it was just the faint whiff of sick) – she let us through to baggage claim. I vow that I will never walk through Border Control without a firm handle on my children's dates of birth ever again.

CHAPTER FOURTEEN

Futureproofing

As part of a married couple with children the future feels easy to plan. Your trajectory is set in stone, a story told by many a Hollywood movie, British sitcom or friends on your cul-de-sac.

You work hard to get on a series of what seem to be progressively slippery ladders: career, property, pension, saving where you can for the ultimate family dream – a holiday to Disney World Florida. Whichever part of the country you reside in, your life no doubt revolves around school or nursery runs, meal planning, catchment areas, family weekend lunches at the local and intermarital spats over who left the wet towel on the bed. You deal with the curveballs life throws at you as a couple, a Taylor Swift-esque squad, swerving each and every one with tears and teamwork, growing firmer family roots by the day.

But when one parent departs from a marriage, the very core – the heartbeat – of your family life is changed completely and irrevocably, never to return to the way it once was.

As a married optimist (and, to be honest, as a new parent who desperately wanted to celebrate the successes where she bloody well could, even if the successes were found simply in everyone being dressed by midday), I took pleasure in rejoicing in each and every little occasion that crossed my path. Mother's Day, Christmas Day, a Wednesday after everyone's slept through the night . . . I just loved to raise a glass or host a dinner to say 'Hooray!' (subtext: we've made it through another twenty-four hours, let's celebrate). But when I became a single mum these celebrations took on a whole new meaning and the milestone days often left me feeling hollow and empty.

I can't really remember my first Mother's Day as a single parent, probably because it was so unremarkable. The kids were too young to go to the toilet on their own, so they certainly weren't hot-footing it up to John Lewis to buy me a gift of a nice Emma Bridgewater mug, or hefting the toaster out of the cupboard to grill a slice of artisanal sourdough to be served to me alongside a cup of tea in bed. The day certainly wasn't the one I'd become briefly used to, the celebration of myself, the mother, where I'd be treated to a lie-in, a bunch of flowers and a long bath. To be honest, on my first single Mother's Day I just wanted to wake up having had more than four hours' sleep and for nobody to wee or poo on me. It's good to aim high.

I did get a breakfast that day: I met my friend Amy at Buddy's, a faux-American diner off the A5 (oh! The glamour of motherhood) for pancakes, waffles and strong coffee. Her fiancé was working away in America so we made the perfect pair . . . I was the pissed-off single mum and she was the work-widow, disgruntled at having to make her own tea on a mother's most sacred day of all.

Despite my (barely concealed) misery, I remember feeling a sense of empowerment on that day, thinking about all the women I knew who were raising families alone. I'd spent a long time anticipating how awful the day was going to be and, though it wasn't the wonderful day of mum-worshipping that I'd been used to, it really wasn't all that bad. As with many things in the world of the single mum, my own societal prejudice and chip on my shoulder caused me more stress and worry than if I'd just let that all go and gone with the flow of our overpriced A5 breakfasting.

The first Mother's Day was done, but the first solo Christmas was still to come. This was, and continues to be, one of the most horrific things about single-parenting, and something I wish I'd argued completely differently for when I was negotiating the custody of my children.

I have friends who have divorced since who concur with this: I know one woman who shares 50/50 custody of her son yet refuses to part from him on Christmas Day. She looked at me agog and aghast when I told her I'd conceded that Will could have the children for half of the Christmases now we were no longer together.

The fact that he moved two and a half hours away made the situation perhaps trickier than it might have been. In an ideal world we'd both spend time with the children on Christmas Day, but literally nobody wants to be in the car on Jesus's birthday when they could be at home stuffing their faces with turkey, Quality Street and Baileys. Me included.

And so we decided we'd split the Christmases 50/50 – one on, one off – with the children spending around four days with each parent before being transported to the other. New Year's Eves would generally be my domain as Will usually had to work these – fine with me; who wants to pay through the nose to spend New Year's Eve in a cramped pub or restaurant when you've got nobody to kiss at midnight? Give me *Jools Holland's Hootenanny* and the fireworks on TV any day of the week.

Well. I'd never truly known despair and sadness until I'd been forced to spend Christmas without my kids. It wasn't just awful . . . it was truly terrible.

Everyone knows that Christmas is all about the children. We're not a religious family, so to us the day pretty much revolves around gifts, togetherness and cheese, but as soon as Elfie came along an aspect of magic was added in to the mix. All of a sudden Christmases were entirely different; I started planning our meals and gifts months in advance, squirrelling toys around the house and plotting which decorations would look best. I acquired a sodding Elf on the Shelf and assorted festive onesies, for fuck's sake – if that's not properly getting into the spirit then I'm not sure what is. But Christmas with children is *so much better* than Christmas without them, so spending Christmas as a mother, but separately from my children, was bloody torture.

I have discovered weird ways of coping without Elfie and Hux on Christmas Day. In my five years of single parenting I've done it twice, and in the lead-up I've found that the best way to cope was to (bah humbug) not buy a Christmas tree: the first time I did this I lived in a tiny house with children who didn't seem to know or care much about non-drop Norway Spruces, and I moved to a new house some nine days before the second solo Christmas, so everyone forgave me my lack of tree. Job done.

Not buying a tree is literally the only way of finding any semblance of pretending to cope, though. Even my parents were away the last time I found myself childless on Christmas day and so, not wanting to join them at my auntie's house and bed down in a sleeping bag on the floor in the spare room at the age of thirty-one, I stayed at home, joining the family for lunch later. It was as awful as it sounds, probably as awful as the sleeping bag would have been.

I woke up on Christmas morning to an empty house. It was just like any morning, only it wasn't, it was Christmas morning, and I felt so lonely I could have screamed. Staying away from the television and any social media (having to look at happy families on that day would have sent me over the edge), I instead went back to sleep for as long as I could without permanently fusing myself to my bed before taking a two-hour bath and driving to Leamington Spa for lunch with my family, which was that year followed by my date in London with philandering Media Mogul John. And we all know how that turned out. Happy Christmas to me!

I cried many times during that day. I cried when I first woke up, I cried when I went back to sleep, I cried when I had a bath, I cried when I drove down to Leamington, I cried going to the loo in the middle of dinner, I cried FaceTiming my children, I cried driving down to London. You could say it was not the merriest of festive days for me.

Having spent all my married Decembers working like a maniac to make sure everyone (apart from myself, usually) had a good time – the hours spent slaving over the home-made mince pies I'd never eat (vom) and the 3 a.m. visits on Christmas Eve to the twenty-four-hour Tesco ('At least it'll be quiet then!' I'd trill to a sleeping house) – it was a very weird feeling to be left alone over Christmas. Keeping myself busy was a difficult task; one year I booked in for a Brazilian wax in a quest to find something, anything that would be more painful than being without my children (it wasn't). And I missed the most ridiculous things about the festive season, like the wide-open space by the back door where the tray containing the reindeer's carrots and Santa's glass of red wine normally sat. Even though I despise the things, I even missed heaving after I took a faux mouthful out of Father Christmas's mince pie as 'proof' that he'd visited.

Sure, I could spend my childless Christmas Eves down the pub if I wanted, but why would I? All my friends were at home reading *The Night Before Christmas* with their own children, gazing out of the window to try to spot Santa's sleigh flying through the sky – or, the more modern version, tracking him on the NORAD iPad app. And yes, I had a quiet lunch and got festively sozzled with other adults; but I would happily have traded that in for the experience of forcing a small child to eat their sprouts or getting clocked in the face with a brand-new Father Christmas-delivered Buzz Lightyear.

Single Christmases were never the same, either. There's something undeniably nuclear about Christmas Day, something about it that seems tailor-made for two parents and their children, not an imbalanced family of three like mine.

But I've found that in so many facets of life that I've faced with just myself and the kids. In conversation, when people found out I was a single parent I could always see their opinion of me changing in that split second.

'I'm sorry,' they'd say, as if I'd just announced I was a recent widow. I could feel their pity radiating off them.

'It must be hard?' they'd enquire.

At the beginning I would always answer in the terrified affirmative, finding nothing scarier than the prospect of my life ahead of me as a single parent.

But then, a couple of years in, my attitude (and reaction) changed.

'It's actually fine,' I'd say. 'We're a team. There might be only three of us but we're still a family.'

And we were. Once all the diary management and juggling of child paraphernalia was sorted (luckily this part got easier as the children grew older and had less need for bottles/nappies/ the kitchen sink when we were out of the house), it really was as easy as just getting through each day. Aside from the odd wish for a Netflix partner or someone else to get up with the kids at 5 a.m. on a Sunday, I really didn't long for a partner much. I didn't even miss sex, knowing I could do it better myself than could any of the men I'd trusted enough to sleep with since my divorce.

I could always tell that the people who enquired about my single-parent status thought the worst thing about my situation was the logistical and perhaps financial issues. 'How do you cope when times are bad?' they'd ask.

The truth was that it wasn't the terrible times when I really missed a partner, a father, but the good ones, the times when I'd realise what incredibly special and clever children mine were. I could do the parents' evenings and nativity plays alone; it wasn't a problem – but I didn't want to. I missed having that one person sat next to me who would squeeze my hand as our child stood up to narrate the story of Mary and Joseph, or one who'd glow with me as we were told how brilliantly our offspring could do joined-up handwriting. I wanted to celebrate the successes of the fruit of my loins with a man who loved them as much as I did, who would think the fact that our youngster had got through a day of nursery without weeing on themselves was as brilliant as I did. I so missed someone who'd recognise the wonderful in the mundanity of our child-rearing, who'd see genius in a two-times-table song or a correctly listed alphabet.

That, alongside the solo decision-making, was something that was difficult to come to terms with. According to researchers at Cornell University the average adult makes around 35,000 conscious decisions a day, and I'd wager that number shoots northwards of ooh, perhaps 100,000 after you give birth to a child that you have to keep warm, fed and alive each day (sidenote: you need a licence to drive a car but not to look after a child. How on earth does that work?!) At times the pressure simply to decide what the whole family was going to eat for breakfast, lunch and dinner was insane, let alone any decision-making I'd have to do over the most suitable nurseries, schools and catchment areas. And it didn't stop there: when I became a single parent every little thing in the household became my decision, from the colour of the curtains hanging at the windows to the weekend family activities I'd arrange, to which mobile phone provider I should use and how many after-school activities I should crowbar the children into doing. It was *exhausting*, necessary but exhausting.

And I have never felt more accomplished.

I decided to stay where I was, in Milton Keynes, for the fore-seeable future, not having any more attractive (or affordable) options at my fingertips. Yes, neighbouring Northampton and Bedford were slightly cheaper, but MK was attractive in its convenience if in no other ways – it's true what they say about the concrete and roundabouts.

I had my parents close by and the lovely bond they shared with the children was invaluable; plus the fact that they saved me a fortune in babysitting fees was a godsend and, to be honest, having spent my teens and early twenties moving all over the country: from Worcestershire to uni in Nottingham down to London and then up to a village near my parents, I was starting to enjoy the familiarity of the place. And the one thing MK naysayers always joke about is the fact that though it's not a sexy city it is easy to escape – the kind of gentle natural disaster that causes the rail services to panic (such as a bit of wind or an inch of snow) notwithstanding, you're only ever a thirty-minute train ride from London.

After my New-York-based Aiden disaster, I spent a while thinking about where I wanted to live, where I'd want to set down roots for ever. NYC was the natural choice: the city I loved the most, the place I returned to year on year. I knew enough people there to generate a marketing and blog income and had become scrappy (read: ambitious) enough to make a success of my life, wherever that might be.

But bloody hell, have you seen the immigration require-ments for America? I'd sooner be sentenced to a life with sudoku as my only hobby than try to decipher getting into

America as a skilled immigrant. My mind boggled at the financial and legal requirements. I knew it would be hard to get a job over there as a single mum with two kids when I lived in the UK, so I looked at going down the freelance route. However, I didn't want to blow £20,000 on a visa lawyer and housing down payments for a life that might or might not work out for us: that's enough for a wedding, a mortgage deposit, a car. I might like to live life slightly on the edge – if the edge is really rather safe and maybe has somewhere soft to fall either side – but there was no way I could justify spending that amount of money on such a risk.

And so Milton Keynes it was. It may not have been what I had spent the last ten years of my life aspiring to but it was home, and who wants to live in a massive palace in Hampstead and send their kids to a private school when you've got the lovely community of David Lloyd MK nearby and within the catchment area of one of the best schools in the county?

I finally started to feel truly settled in my life about three years after Will left our home. It took that long for me to finally relax at places like the school gate, somewhere that had previously been a location of fear and nerves for me. I was never a natural 'mummy' – I always said the only children I really liked were my own (though there have been some notable exceptions, like my friend Bryony's gorgeous daughters) – and I believed my discomfort was there on my face for all to see, for them all to judge the young mum who didn't belong at the school gates. Of course, that was pretty much nonsense and I now participate in the same PTA meetings and events I used to be shit scared of. But still, it took me a long time to get there.

Soon, I started to feel like things were starting to come together. My children were brilliant, I really liked my job, I was getting more sleep. I felt so full of life, love and accomplishment that the instances of cheaters and ghosters were a distant memory, something I'd left well in the past.

And then I met a man.

CHAPTER FIFTEEN

Heartbreak Lessons

I meet Steve at the gym which, if we were both gay men existing inside an episode of Lena Dunham's GIRLS, would have made us a sitcom-worthy cliché. I'd joined our local David Lloyd some 3 years previous on recommendation from my mother, as according to her I needed to have somewhere to socialise, to meet people that weren't work colleagues or other women on the other end of my Instagram. *At the very least* I thought, eyeing up the mini soft play in the corner of the café *it'll give me somewhere to drink wine while the children tire themselves out.*

Out-and-out refusing to go to the quarterly over 30s discos held at the Heath Club (I might be tragic but not quite singles disco-level tragic) it took about a year before I started to thaw enough to speak to my fellow gym-goers. Working for myself I spent a lot of time in the club's business lounge, and I was intrigued by a tall, dark and handsome older man I used to see on the tennis courts daily. He was never with a woman, didn't seem to keep normal working hours and had an incredible level of fitness. I started to expect his presence during my bi-weekly sanity saving gym trips

(God bless that soft play) and, though we'd never interacted, when he's not around I felt weirdly disappointed.

I speak to Steve for the first time about a year after I notice him. The club's café had just been refurbished and I'm there for a coffee after a long night with the kids: I order an Americano which takes ages to arrive and as a typical hating-to-complain Brit I hem and haw to myself, muttering my annoyance under my breath without moaning out loud to anyone who might actually be able to help. Steve is behind me in the queue and, sensing my exasperation, makes a comment – which escapes me now – causing me to smile and thaw slightly. Wondering why the tall handsome man has spoken to me I go hot in the face, wishing him a nice day before scurrying into the business lounge to do some work. I have butterflies.

Steve doesn't wear a wedding ring so I don't realise the man I exchange polite and anonymous pleasantries with weekly is married until someone tells me. Despite never having experienced anything more than small talk with him I'm disappointed; he has something about him that made me want to find out more – he gives me a feeling that he is someone I should get to know better. But I don't, not wanting to stoop to the philandering lows of Married Mike or Media Mogul John, and I go back to my life of climbing the slippery career ladder while being disappointed by everyone I meet from Tinder and Bumble.

Another six months later and the gym grapevine is alight with talk that Steve and his wife have separated. I tell him I'm sorry to hear that (I'm not) and go along with my day.

It's another six months before we connect again, six months where I've been mucked around literally from the other side of the world. Incensed by my latest love life failure I arrive at the gym one Thursday, and striding out to the cross trainer I catch Steve's eye out the corner of mine and decide to walk towards him instead. I ask how he is. 'Not great', he tells me. 'I've had a pretty shit week, actually'.

I nod in assent, 'Me too!' I affirm. 'Must be something in the water'.

In a fit of uncharacteristic confidence I decide to do something I've never done before and ask him out. Well, kind of. 'You can take me out for dinner, you know,' I say. I can tell he's slightly taken aback with how forward I've been.

'That would be nice,' he says. I give him my phone number and head off to the gym equipment to let off a little bit of steam.

We go out the next Saturday and I'm not sure what to make of it. Is it a romantic date? Is it two friends getting together for drinks and dinner date? Do I like him? Does he like me?

I'd spent the morning carefully curling my hair and I hop in my pre-ordered taxi as soon as it arrives, feeling a mixture of excitement and apprehension. But, as we're almost at the train station fifteen minutes away, beauty-based disaster strikes. 'I don't know if I turned my hair tongs off!' I announce to my eye-rolling taxi driver. 'We've got to turn back!'

We turn around, I check them (they're off, of course they're bloody off) and I re-start my journey into London. If I'm anxious enough to be imagining my hair tongs burning a hole through my dressing table I must be nervous for the date (or non-date, whatever).

I'm forty-five minutes late, embarrassed and flustered, but Steve is the perfect gentleman. Meeting in the bar at the Covent

Garden Hotel he'd ordered a couple of cocktails, letting me pick which of the two I'd like when I arrive. I chose the rhubarb one, taking a slurp as I apologise profusely. He's completely charming and tells me not to worry. At a later date he will tell me I thought I looked like a supermodel walking in: Kate Moss I am not but I adore that he loves me so much he says things like that.

Leaving the bar we stroll through the tourist-filled streets to J. Sheekey, an old-school seafood restaurant close to Leicester Square. We sit down for dinner and I drink a glass of champagne, feeling happily like a queen in such beautiful surroundings with a handsome and interesting man opposite me. I'm not nervous any more, just happy this situation isn't as cringy and awkward as it could have been, so we order and settle into an evening in each other's company. About an hour in to the meal I look across at him and stop him mid-conversation: 'Steve', I say, 'I'm having a really wonderful evening. Thank-you.'

Our relationship begins tentatively and is not without turbulence. We have a twenty-two-year age gap, which caused much gossip and consternation (HELLO Catherine Zeta-Jones and Michael Douglas, Beyoncé and Jay-Z, Calista Flockhart and Harrison Ford . . . we'd be just another couple if we lived in LA rather than MK) and it hurt to be called names and had to defend myself against accusations of having the wrong motivations in our relationship. Then there were our respective children to consider – his are adult age and, like mine, live with him – so together we were toting more than a small amount of luggage along with us for the ride. That being said it all seemed to fit into place.

Despite having referred to one or two men in the last couple of years as my 'boyfriend', this is the first situation where I've felt like I'm in a relationship. I've been let down plenty of times since being divorced but have never truly let myself be vulnerable, not wanting to open my heart and mind to the act of love, of letting someone else hold such a huge part of my happiness. Even now, with five years of single life under my belt, I catch myself often in fight or flight mode, so terrified am I of being in a place where everything about me is so beholden to another person.

Our relationship isn't easy and is a short sharp lesson in the fact it probably shouldn't be. In my teens and twenties I was always guilty of believing that our biggest challenge in life was finding love but I now realise this isn't true: the most difficult part is cherishing the love we have, making sure those we treasure are able to blossom and be happy in the relationships we share. I put my learnings on this partly down to my marriage, for sure, but also thank my children for the lessons they've taught me, too.

Before I became I mother I saw marriage as a bit of an end game, a pinnacle you reach after weeks, months or years of searching down the person you were supposed to spend your life with. I always felt lucky that I'd found my forever partner in Will, and by settling down at such a young age I believed because I'd met and married a man that I no longer needed to work at our relationship, my family or myself. In my mind marriage was it: I believed we were perfect as we were and all we had to do post-wedding was wait until we lived happily ever after – I had no inkling that self-reflection and understanding of us as a couple was required or even recommended.

Which I guess is why we didn't communicate, I didn't work as hard at being a good person as I should have. I didn't make enough (or any, really) effort at making him happy over my just *being*, which is all I thought I had to do as a married woman.

Wrong.

Having my children totally changed my perspective on love. All of a sudden I had two little people whose lives totally depended on me, I had to sacrifice so much of what I was – including my nipples, my sleep and my flat stomach – to make them happy. And this was non-negotiable, whether I liked it or not. Come hell or high water I was going to become selfless, be a better person.

This realisation was too late for my marriage but is something I think about often when it comes to my new partnerships. I might not want to surrender my entire happiness to another person, rely on them for my purpose in life, but I do want to be the best person I can possibly be. It's something I muse on the daily: what is the point of life if we're not constantly striving for the A1 version of ourselves? Why would you be mean when you could be kind? In matters of the heart, I resolved, I would be the light in someone else's life. As long as they wouldn't extinguish my own.

Steve and I dove head-first into a relationship where we shouldn't have. I was wide open to falling in love, ready to put into practice my preceding years of self-development and realisations, wanting to generate only happiness and security for someone else, the way I always believed a fulfilling and happy relationship would be. But I didn't take into account the fact that Steve, fresh out of a twenty-something marriage and with a generous amount of familial and emotional housekeeping to take care of, might not be ready for it. I ploughed on regardless.

In the year I spent with Steve I learned an incredible amount about how much I've changed since my marriage. Now, self-identifying as a feminist, I realised this mind-set encompassed not just the woman I was at work but the role I wanted to take in relationships, too. And the biggest arguments I had in this coupling always revolved around times Steve gave me his opinions on decisions and ideas that I felt he should have nothing to do with: the clothes I wore, the books I read, the friends I drank too many cocktails with. As far as I was concerned, if I wanted to wear a bikini to do the supermarket shop whilst reading the most sexually explicit book and WhatsApping my craziest single girlfriend, that was my shout. And although I am yet to wander the organic veg with a bare midriff, retaining my agency and self-belief is one of the most important things to me in a relationship – it won't be removed.

I never called Steve my other half and still cringe when I hear others referring to their partners in that way. Steve was part of my team, he was my partner and I loved him a huge amount. But I was still whole without him, and that knowledge made me feel more secure than in any other relationship I'd been in previously. I'd stayed in my marriage for longer than I should have because I was scared of who I would be outside of it – I think this is how many people in on-the-rocks relationships feel – but the last five years have taught me that I don't need a man to feel whole. I don't need a man to raise my kids. And I don't need a man to be financially comfortable – single women are able to do a pretty good job of all that on our own. A man is something I want to have to enhance my already happy life, but I'm comfortable in the fact that the days are sunny enough without an owner of a penis in them.

Steve and I got engaged just over six months into our relationship, which felt like a very natural progression. We were in love, yes, but it also felt like we had something to prove, like we needed to show the naysayers that our relationship was valid and happy, and that nothing they could say would split us apart. Which was all well and good until the pressures of said naysayers and a messy divorce process did just that: having known only amicability with my own ex-husband, and a divorce that at its worst point was only slightly uncomfortable, it was both an eye-opening and tough pill to swallow. The stress of the situation was immense, and I was just a bystander, a chorus member. I lost both hair and sleep, spending nights tossing and turning at the thought of the people out there who were casting judgements and spewing vitriol in my direction, all because I'd fallen in love with a man who was six months in to a marriage separation.

Considering breaking up this relationship was, again, scary. But through the fear I had a certainty I'd never known before, a comfort that told me I'd be OK: even if Steve and I parted ways I knew I'd be happy and I'd thrive once more as a single woman, I'd achieve on my own. And that certainty is what made me confident enough to end my engagement, to call time on the relationship with Steve when I knew in my heart of hearts that it just wasn't right. I loved him but I didn't love the way the relationship was making me feel, and I needed to prioritise my own happiness again.

That didn't make it easy, though. Being so much more in tune with my emotions made this conscious decision to end the relationship incredibly difficult, and left me in a place I hadn't been before. I didn't have babies to pull myself together for this time, I didn't have to hide my sadness from my friends and family. I went with it full-pelt, spending days crying uncontrollably, sobbing over mentions of his name or songs we listened to together.

I knew I'd hit rock bottom one Friday. It was 1pm and I was still in my pyjamas with un-brushed teeth, having eaten nothing but cake that day. I had pressing work deadlines but instead had spent the morning watching the entire three hours and thirty-seven minutes of Prince William's wedding on YouTube, while sobbing into bits of loo roll. I got up to replenish my tissues and caught a glimpse of my greasy hair and spotty chin in the mirror and thought – enough now.

It was a bank holiday weekend and I granted myself that time to feel sorry for myself – the wallowing, red wine consumption and shower-swerving were quite normal post-breakup, I said – but come Tuesday I'd be plunging back into the real world. The world of work deadlines, washing and happiness. The world of the real people, the ones who might not be in relationships but were happy and successful all the same. My world.

Having It All

CHAPTER SIXTEEN

Having It All

Despite such an incredibly difficult break-up and far too many occasions that I ate cake for breakfast, I'm really happy that I'm not finishing this book on the 'happily ever after' of an engagement.

Because although we are no longer together I'd still be happy if I wasn't in a relationship. Happiness is not found in a fellow human with whom you have a relationship but in a huge other number of things: our families, our children, our friendships and our work. And, in my opinion, taking the focus away from that one major relationship and realising you are a singular person – not defined by the one you're with – allows all the other parts of your life to flourish.

Hand on heart I can say that one of the toughest lessons I learned from the break-up of my marriage was the realisation that I'd put all my metaphorical friendship eggs, the ones that existed outside of my marriage, in one basket. I'd gone through a couple of big cross-country moves with my husband and those relocations, coupled with the tricky life events we'd navigated together as a couple, meant I'd left my friendships either in another city or completely by the wayside. That's not to say I was a complete friendless recluse; I always had someone to go for a glass of wine with (essential), but I didn't feel like I had many friend relationships that were anywhere near as nourishing and close as my marriage. And so I just didn't really bother treating them with the respect they deserved.

This pressure on a partnership that lacked the sounding board of female friendship definitely contributed to the demise of my marriage. Will was always my closest confidant, the person I'd note as my in-case-of-emergency, and despite how awesome it was to put all my trust in this one person I found I had nobody away from him to talk to about my relationship – or, when we started breaking down, about everything else. I've always been close to my mum and should have leaned on her more, but confiding that my marriage wasn't as OK as it seemed to someone who was such an intrinsic part of my family, and by extension my marriage, felt like a betrayal.

Attending village baby groups, I felt forcibly pushed together with the women I met, the women I was expected to forge a friendship with just because we were all mothers. I was happy to exchange pleasantries with them, discuss weaning and ask for nursery recommendations, but our relationships never reached higher heights than the sharing of tepid cups of church-hall tea. I never felt comfortable enough with them to touch on my ailing marriage or even my experiences with post-natal depression.

But then I started to form a friendship with Kaisa, a power-house who I met on Twitter. She was an outgoing and gregarious journalist who'd gone from working for *Elle* magazine to having kids and moving to the countryside, much like me, and she now owned a small clothing shop in the village we both lived in. Her incredibly confident nature and sharp sense of style were intimidating to me when we first met: she dressed in the most effortlessly chic Scandinavian clothes while I slobbed around in variations on Primark Breton tops and baggy leggings, but I think we saw in each other glimmers of recognition. We'd both had careers and had given them up to pursue our family lives, and perhaps both felt a little resentful of the businesses and social lives our husbands now enjoyed while we stayed at home and awaited their return every day.

There were so many parallels in our situations that Kaisa soon became one of my closest friends, someone I felt I could confide in. I would rock up at her shop on a Friday afternoon, baby in sling, and we'd share a couple of glasses of prosecco as we cackled over the stories of our week, regaling each other with tales of our respective lives. We talked about our marriages and wondered how we'd got from A to B, how we'd come to find ourselves in relationships that felt like they were failing fast despite the children who, surely, should be the glue that held us together. I deduced from my prosecco Fridays with Kaisa that this was now my life, this was just the way a marriage was supposed to work. If my exuberant, ambitious and talented friend felt at as much of a dead end as I did with the man she'd said 'I do' to, what hope did I have?

A year after I'd met Kaisa I reached breaking point and Will and I split. Kaisa and her husband broke up about six months later. It turned out that both of us weren't completely at a dead end; we just needed to adjust our routes to not include our husbands.

Kaisa is now one of the most kick-ass single mums I know. Not only does she totally own the fact that she parents three lovely kids solo, but she's a mega-successful personal trainer and is the strongest woman I've ever met – literally; she can lift weights that I can't even look at. We've both come a long way since prosecco Fridays.

I haven't purposely chosen to be friends with other single mums but it seems that we have automatically gravitated towards each other. Carlina is another one, an ex-colleague who I always hugely respected but who, as she was a couple of levels senior to me in our roles at *VICE*, was never someone I thought of as friendship material. She was poised, savvy and strong: again, I was intimidated by her confidence, her commercial nous and, to be honest, her clothes. After leaving *VICE* – me for Milton Keynes and Carlina for Southampton – she and I were just Facebook friends and communicated nothing beyond the odd 'Happy Birthday!' or 'Congratulations!' on each other's wall. But we reconnected shortly before she split from her husband.

After initially bonding over my experiences and her expectations of divorce, we have become the closest friends and her care, thoughtfulness and taste for a great bottle of wine have been so important to me over the last year. We spend evenings on the phone nattering over our latest man happenings, hours during the day sending each other inspirational Pinterest quotes (God, how #basic), and I couldn't love the friendship any more. Five years ago her seniority would have meant I would have kept her at arm's length, not wanting to engage past the superficial pleasantries, but now we talk about everything: periods, relationships, kids, hopes, dreams, business. Carlina has helped me realise that female friendship is not just ace, it's necessary, and I'm excited to see how our relationship develops.

Then there are the married friends I have, the ones whose company I would have previously enjoyed at dinner parties and playdates but never taken further than the shallows. I have Néva, who loves my children almost as much as I do (probably because she can give them back), and whose years of measured friendship have always been so comforting. I will always remember her texting me when she realised my relationship with Shaun was getting serious:

Be careful with your heart precious girl,

she told me,

it is fragile.

She makes me feel so loved and cared for in an unconditional way I have never felt from a woman, I can't even explain it.

Then there's Bryony, my absolute parenting role model, who I hold in such high esteem when it comes to marriage and kids. She's my no-nonsense down-the-line friend, the one who will tell me things straight, no matter how difficult I might find her words. Everyone needs a Bryony in their life: her advice is valuable and her approval is priceless.

But my experiences of female friendship have not all been

girly pow-wows and squeals over who gets to be Carrie in our *Sex and the City*-ish monthly London dinner get-togethers. The relationships I've forged with the women in my life have been some of the most precious but also the most destructive of all. Though I've cried my share of tears over the times I've been messed around or ghosted by men who married the women they cheated on me with (OK, so this has only happened the once, but it still made me feel like I was living an episode of *EastEnders*), the most painful relationship break-up of all has been one with a female.

You'll remember Kate, the friend I went to visit in New York: the one who picked me up when my marriage was going south, the person I wanted to celebrate my thirtieth birthday with, the girl I jokingly referred to as my BFF (but I meant it). Shortly after Aiden deserted me for Deanna, she did exactly the same thing and disappeared – poof – as if in a cloud of smoke.

I wish I could tell you why, how or what happened, but in all honesty I can't quite remember.

I hate to blame any aspect of my life or indeed this relationship breakdown on being a single parent, but sometimes I just have to hold my hands up and say, do you know what – being the sole caretaker to two kids and, oh yeah, the only person who earns a crust in my house? It's really time-consuming and stressful and I often need my friends to give me a bit of a nudge and say 'Oi! Remember me! Come out from your work-and-kids-fug and drink wine with me.' And I love them for it.

I wonder if this is what went wrong with Kate. I wonder if she was pissed off with me about something – I'm not sure what, but I suspect she felt like I neglected her on the trip I took to New

York in favour of Aiden, despite us spending every single day together (and let's not forget that I spent a day out of that five-day holiday helping her move house). Anyway, she has never told me what happened. She just stopped replying to my text messages and in my single-parent busyness I just didn't notice.

As we all do in these situations, I sensed something was wrong and left Kate to sort whatever was going on, decompress for a while; this usually resolved any issues we had in our friendship, but that time we simply never came back from it. I didn't hear from Kate but I was so busy with life, work and children that by the time I stopped to think and realised she hadn't responded to my latest text messages or reached out to me herself, it almost felt too late. And then I realised that she'd deleted me from her Instagram friends and from Facebook too, the ultimate millennial kick in the teeth; I was incredibly hurt but at the same time it had been so long that I felt foolish for not noticing her silence previously. I thought we'd come to a place where I couldn't be the one to reach out myself. I kick myself for that now.

Do I blame myself for the friendship breakdown? I'm not sure. I can't say that I did anything wrong, and certainly nothing that would deserve a flounce of such epic proportions, but I can't say categorically that I didn't offend her, either. She was my best friend and I would have hoped that if I'd done something to hurt her so much that she didn't want to speak to me any more she could have just told me so; but I know from experience that sometimes we're just too mad or upset to be rational when it comes to those we're closest to.

I'd thought we were close enough to avoid situations like this, though: I wasn't religious but I'd anointed her honorary godparent to my son, we'd slept in the same bed, we'd shared secrets that neither of us had disclosed to anyone else. Her disappearance hurt and amidst all the forgotten nonsense from the men in my life I have dated, it is the one emotional scar that I return to time and time again, only I try not to because it is just too awful. I miss her horribly.

You see, the men, they know how to execute a disappearing act *Road Runner*-style, but it's the women who I will remember for ever. What are those terrible sayings? Fries before guys, chicks before dicks? You probably have to be ten years younger than me to utter them out loud (or re-pin them to your Pinterest board) but the end of my friendship with Kate was definitely a lesson in their deeper meaning.

Five years on from divorce and despite me being what feels like a legitimate Independent Woman – I listen to Beyoncé and Destiny's Child now far more than is probably normal – I like spending time with men. In my time as a single woman I have never been worried about being a spinster: I'm sure I could have got a house rabbit, a dog, a rare-breed cat, and been pretty happy attending my children's university graduations solo with only my crazy animal-woman persona for company.

Nor did I spend an inordinate amount of time worrying that my vagina would seal over and I'd suddenly develop a taste for clashing patterned curtains and carpets, because I truly believe that spinsterhood and single mum-hood is most definitely not the worst thing that can happen to a woman.

Though I'd bet that, if divorce is something you're about to embark on (or are thinking of embarking on) right now, you won't be able to see that. You'll be scared, you'll be worried, you'll feel a serious lack of self-confidence. You *definitely* won't think you can do it.

Tentatively stretching your wings to experience a life alone is the scariest thing you can do after spending a portion of your life as a man's partner, and contemplating branching out from that, especially when you have children, is a terrifying prospect.

And can I tell you something? That's exactly how I felt – and is in fact still how I sometimes feel. Becoming a single mum places so much responsibility on you that you've never before shouldered alone. It relies on you being a good parent, bringing in the money, having the diary-management skills to rival the most competent executive PA. When I think now about everything single-parenting entails I seriously want to lie down and either weep or take a big nap (speaking of which, naps are one of the most important weapons in your artillery; don't be afraid to use them) and occasionally I still do this, but of course only until school pick-up time.

We are not defined by the love of our partner, we are not on this planet to serve them as 'wife'. We are here to raise the next generation to be brilliant and, not only that, to be brilliant ourselves, which sometimes might mean showing our children that hey, your mummy is the strongest woman you've ever met. Because even though you might not feel that way when your husband is halfway out the door, or boning his admin assistant, or spending the money you've carefully saved for Brownie camp on beer down the local: YOU ARE. We are. I've never met a mother who isn't warm, resourceful and switched-on enough to make a life for her family, and whether or not you have a bloke in your life that is the most important thing to know. You can do whatever you want to do and a man shouldn't stop you.

Your kids will cry, they will shout at you, they will spend some nights vomiting on you as if you never gave up your job, sanity or boobs to make them happy. But, whether you're married or not, they will grow up thinking you are the bee's knees, the most brilliant person on the planet, just as you will go through adulthood knowing your kids are the purpose of your being.

And what a very special gift that is to be given.

Acknowledgements

This book would never be in existence without my marriage, so a huge thank-you to my ex-husband Will who has always been an incredibly good sport when it comes to my inherent need to write about my – and by extension, his – life experiences. Thanks also go to him for giving me Elfie and Hux, the two most special people I've ever met in my entire life. If nothing else, we did them right.

There are many who believed in me much more than I believed in myself throughout this publication process, and the actuality of this book is in huge part thanks to them. One is my agent, Robert Dinsdale at Independent Literary, who signed me all those years ago yet always kept the faith I was just a few weeks away from writing my book deal-winning material (we got there in the end!!). I also owe a huge debt of gratitude to my publisher and editor Charlotte Hardman, who saw enough in my Instagram captions to message me about writing a memoir: those few gently enquiring words got me off my bum to pen the book I've wanted to write ever since I was a little girl.

To my Mum and Dad, who supported me through my efforts to write my first book, Roger and the Ghost (by Alice age 5), and this one, too. My family of three would be nowhere without your love, your wonderful grandparenting and your babysitting. My friend Laura Jane Williams, who has encouraged and championed me from the off, recognising how bloody hard it is to put pen to paper (or fingers to keyboard) when it comes to scribing such a bare-all volume: your cheerleading was, and continues to be, so important. And Jamie Klingler, Queen of the London literary clubs, who read one of the very first drafts of Chapter One six years ago (was that the night I lost my keys?). I can't wait to see my book featured in your 2018 list!

To Claire Cohen, who invited me in to the *Telegraph* and made my dream of writing for a newspaper come true – you gave me more confidence than you will ever know, and I will always be grateful for your belief. I also still think you're one of the best-dressed people in the media.

A huge thanks to my Instagram community and blog readers: I wouldn't be here without you, pure and simple. You picked me up so many times when life really didn't seem All That, and it's down to you all I am so happy today and living a career I love.

To all the men who messed me around over the years: I told you I'd get my revenge. Thanks for the material.

A huge big thank-you to all my friends who were so loving, patient and kind to me, not only when I went AWOL when writing this book but also through my journey during these last five years of life. I will be eternally grateful to you all for showing me what love means, and helping me realise that it doesn't necessarily have to come from a man. Néva, Bryony, Carlina, Claire, Caoimhe, Sarah . . . you have been my best boyfriends and I love you. Who needs a man when you have a girl gang?